What Rea

I read *Write Your Story* not long after I found myself with a book just longing to come out, and no idea how to start. This book gave me a blueprint of where I was going with practical steps and answered questions that I hadn't even thought to ask as an aspiring author. It also gave some much needed encouragement that has kept me from quitting through the process. I also appreciated the section on the possible emotional hurdles, as I could relate to many of them and it was a comfort to know that I wasn't alone. I will be giving this book to others who are interested in writing. - **Jennifer Cabezon, missionary**

I have personally anticipated the release of *Write Your Story*. As an author, I wish I could have read it before I began writing. Betsy's practical wisdom and personal encouragement is exactly what a new writer or author needs. This book is an invaluable resource to help anyone bring their story to life. - **Cathy Harris, author of** *Created to Live: Becoming the Answer for an Abortion-Free Community*

Betsy has a passion to encourage writers to go for it – to push past fear, distraction, and excuses to pursue expression. I believe she even has an anointing that stirs up a desire to write. Sit next to her at your own risk! As she blazed an indie publishing path in her own life, she naturally extended an invitation to those in her sphere to join her on the journey. This book flows from that invitation. *Write Your Story* will be an excellent resource for those who are new to the publishing world. Be encouraged, even exhorted, to draw close to the One who placed that desire within you and *Write Your Story*. - **Gina Green, writer**

After writing my first book, I was a bit overwhelmed with the publication and promotion process. *Write Your Story* gave me some great ideas to expand my readership and actually encouraged me to start writing my next book! - **Julianne Hale, author of** *Covert Awakening*

Write Your Story captures something unique: it is like a "flesh" and "spirit" how-to guide for writing! The "flesh" is the demystifying, practical help for understanding every aspect of writing, editing, publishing, and marketing a book. The "spirit" is the encouragement and hope that Betsy breathes into the book to cause someone to believe that he can and should share his heart through writing! - **Julie Wine, writer and homeschooling mom**

As pastor Ron Lewis says, "There is no romance without finance." Mrs. Herman has done an excellent job of explaining what it takes to get a book finished – and marketed. That last part is where many of us drop the ball – and she has shown me how to get back on the ball. When Johannes Gutenberg made it easier for people to get their ideas into print, the world changed. New technologies make it easier for us to break through the embargoes created by a handful of "official" publishing houses. These are great days to package innovative thinking. As Martin Luther said, "If you want to change the world, pick up your pen and write." So, what are you waiting for? - **Thomas C. Smedley, PhD, adjunct professor at Geneva College and Thomas Edison State University**

I've read a lot of books on writing, indie-publishing, and book marketing. What I appreciate most about Betsy Herman's new book is that she's detailed the practical information and highlighted what's most important for Christian writers. She reminds the reader why we're writing in the first place, and gives us the motivation to keep going should we lose our way or give up all together. I highly recommend this book to anyone who wants to persevere in their God-given gift of writing. - **Suzanne K. Lee, author of** *I Belong*

Write Your Story
Straightforward Steps for (Finally) Writing and Publishing Your Book

Betsy Herman

Copyright © 2018 Betsy Herman

ISBN: 978-0-9983600-1-0
Embracing Hope Publishing

All rights reserved. No portion of this book may be reproduced, except for brief quotations, without the prior written permission of the author.

All Scripture quotations taken from The Holy Bible, New International Version® NIV® Copyright © 1973, 1978, 1984, 2011 by Biblica, Inc.™ Used by permission. All rights reserved worldwide.

Printed in the United States of America

Cover Design: Rebekah Hauck, Peachtree Graphic Designs

Author Photograph: Karen Saunders Photography

Note: Any weblinks mentioned are active at the time of publication.

with thanks to the Unlocking Words community

CONTENTS

Introduction

    Chapter 1: Pioneer

    Chapter 2: Unlocking Words

    Chapter 3: When You Have a Book Idea

    Chapter 4: Sit Down and Write

    Chapter 5: How?

    Chapter 6: These Struggles are Real

    Chapter 7: Editing

    Chapter 8: Who is Your Audience?

    Chapter 9: Getting Real About Finances

    Chapter 10: How Do I Get Published?

    Chapter 11: Marketing and Launching

    Chapter 12: You are an Author!

About the Author

Acknowledgements

Notes and Resources

Other Books by Betsy Herman

Introduction

I hope that by turning these pages you discover more than a book. This is also a map, designed to point you in the right direction as you navigate the process of writing and publishing your own book.

After publishing a couple of books and receiving numerous questions from friends and acquaintances who wanted to write and publish their own books, I began to piece together the process as I understood it. This short book covers more than just the progression of writing and publishing; here you'll also read about some of the emotional and spiritual hurdles that can bog you down.

I am not trying to provide a thorough how-to guide or an instructional manual; as you open these pages you'll find an outline saturated with the affirmation that you can do it! I trust that *Write Your Story* provides you with direction and causes you to grow as a writer, and helps you to evaluate your publishing and marketing options.

These are my reflections about writing a deeply personal memoir, and a glimpse of what it's like to independently publish. Indie publishing (independent publishing) refers to books published without an agent or a publishing company. That is the publishing route I have chosen, but you may consider other options. Technology has made the self-publishing process easier than ever. However, there is a lot more to becoming an author than simply writing.

Write Your Story is intended for Christians, primarily because my faith flows into what I write. You do not have to share my faith to gain insight from this book.

Also, please keep in mind that I write from the United States, so resources I mention might not be available in all countries. The overall ideas will apply to writers throughout the world, but resources may vary from place to place.

If you have a book on your heart and don't know how to take it from idea to finished product, then this book is for you. Whether you end up publishing traditionally or independently, if you're a new author or dream of one day becoming an author, this book will help guide you. I hope that reading about the lessons I've learned and the hurdles I have overcome will equip you to finish strongly.

Chapter 1: Pioneer

As a young child, I sometimes pretended that my bed or my toy wagon in the yard were covered wagons. In my imagination, I was traveling over rustic terrain to settle the Wild West. Stories about the covered wagon days still catch my attention because I like the sense of adventure, the idea of forging a trail, and exploring new places.

Early in my marriage I confessed to my husband that I sometimes wished that I lived in the Laura Ingalls Wilder days. He has since repeatedly reminded me that as much as I enjoy hot showers, a comfortable bed, and the internet, I probably would not have loved settling the west.

He's right. Recently it occurred to me that I never truly wanted to live in a covered wagon. Driving from one end of Virginia to the other in a car makes me feel restless, so I cannot imagine traveling from the East Coast to the Midwest in a canvas-roofed wooden wagon. Let's face it, those trendy tiny houses don't even appeal to me.

Have you noticed that movies and television shows make the lives of writers, bookstore owners and even paper companies seem romantic and exciting? The big screen makes a writer's life seem glamorous, doesn't it?

The lives of writers and settlers might seem exciting, yet the reality is that these things require hard work.

If you picked up this book, it's likely that you're a writer, maybe even one who is struggling to know where to begin. Maybe you're finding the process to be difficult and far from glamorous.

You probably began reading this book because you have an idea, a dream, or a divine calling to write a book, but you don't know where to begin, or you feel overwhelmed by the process.

I'm not going to guarantee that this book will make you famous or show you how to make your fortune by writing books. However, I will suggest ways to publish a book without paying a lot of money up front.

I'm not going to tell you how to write well. There are plenty of manuals and classes for that.

However, if you've ever thought, "I want to write a book someday," then I am going to tell you that your someday can be right now. I'm going to cheer you on and tell you that you can do it. I'm here to share tips that will take you from the first sentence to the finished product.

Let's walk through the writing, editing, publishing, and promoting process from idea to finished project. I'm writing this for you, because I know that you can do it. This book is written from a faith-based perspective, and the practical principles will apply to all.

So, who am I, and why am I qualified to tell you about the writing process? Stick around for a few minutes and take a glimpse into my life. Maybe you're a friend or social media contact and I've said "read this to see if it answers your questions." Maybe you found this book on Amazon In any case, I hope you find some answers here.

Although I don't want to live in a covered wagon, my heart feels more alive when I think about settlers of the west, because I relate to their pioneer spirit. I don't always feel like a pioneer – I'm just a woman who pours her heart into words on a computer screen. I'm just a girl who likes to tell everyone around her that they too can write a book. I'm just a person who gets up and drinks coffee and works a day job and tries to honor God with her life.

But I'm also a pioneer. I'm a trailblazer.

Chances are, if this book appeals to you, you're a pioneer too. You have a message or a story on your heart that you feel compelled to put into words and share with the world. You might feel unqualified. I do too. I question myself as I write this book: who am I to publish a book on writing? I don't have a degree in this subject, and I've only written two books so far.

The more I write, the more I feel convinced that everyone who writes a book is a pioneer. Each of us writes because we have a message, a map for those who follow us, an insight about what we've learned, or a story that is unique. Writers are leaders, even when we feel shy or inadequate.

When you're a trailblazer, you keep going forward. Then, you send a message to those coming behind you to tell them how to follow. You let others know about the best path, and you tell them how to survive when things get tough. A pioneer will tell those who follow them the stories about what they find on the other side. As a forerunner, he or she presses on and leads the way. As an author, and especially as a writer exploring the publishing world and its ever-changing technology, I intend to blaze a trail for you as you write, publish, and share your book.

Chapter 2: Unlocking Words

As numerous people shared with me their ideas of books they want to write but don't know how to publish, I felt as if God gave me the idea to write this how-to book for aspiring Christian authors. *Write Your Story* intends to walk you through the process in a straightforward way. I'll address some of the emotional and spiritual struggles that bogged me down as a new author, with strategies to help you overcome them quickly.

Let me you a little bit about myself, so that you understand my writing background, and maybe you'll even find yourself saying "me too!"

Since learning how to read at a young age, I've been a book-lover. As a child, I dreamed of publishing books one day. When I was eight or ten years old, my siblings and cousins and I regularly produced a family newspaper, and we sold subscriptions. We wrote, printed, and mailed out many issues of *The Hopper Journal*.

As a young teenager, I bought a word processor, which was like a fancy typewriter. In the tenth grade my mom told me I had to take a typing class (do they even offer that in schools today?) I am grateful for her insistence that I learn the practical skill of typing, since twenty years later I am writing books.

I joined the newspaper staff in high school, serving as a co-editor during my senior year. I learned how to write concisely, and I learned how to lay out words on a page in a way that appeals to the reader. Formatting skills are important to any blogger or self-published author, so I am grateful for that foundation.

In college, I spent one year serving on the school newspaper as the Spiritual Life editor. At our Christian college we had a Spiritual Life section of our monthly newspaper. I remember feeling like this was an outlet where I could do what I felt called to do: write about matters of faith. However, I was a bit silly in college, and I titled my column "Prunes for the Spiritually Constipated." Pardon the toilet humor, but I can see how that title still fits me today as I try to encourage people to become unstuck in areas of hope and writing.

Writing about faith comes naturally, since I come from a long line of people who write and paint, but I also have a substantial family heritage of pastors and missionaries. Faith-based writing is not just a calling I discovered in college, it's part of my DNA. I want to people overcome when I'm encouraging women to start *Embracing Hope During Infertility* or when I'm helping fellow Christians write the books that are on their hearts.

After college, I needed a job that paid the bills, so dreams of writing were pushed aside for a while. However, in the age of dial-up internet, my friends introduced me to this idea called Xanga, something we referred to as our "online journals" where we would write stuff on the internet. Mine was called Orange Rhino, named after an incident where I found myself dangling by my jacket from a piece of modern art in Asheville, North Carolina. My Orange Rhino online journal was the beginning of my blogging.

I learned an important lesson from the Orange Rhino, back in the early days of the internet. At that time, I worked for our local 911 dispatch center. That role was one of the most exciting jobs I've ever had. However, in that small town, it was a small world, even on the internet. Police officers would often stop by the 911 center to chat, and one day a police office said to me, "So, I hear you like bossing cops around."

I'm sure my body experienced every nervous reaction at that moment. I was thinking something along the lines of, "Oh no!

How did he read my online journal?" I had posted those exact words about my job on the world wide web. It turned out that his wife had been reading someone else's posts, and as she clicked through friends of friends, she came across my posts, and asked her husband, "Do you know a dispatcher named Betsy?" He was amused, yet still gracious. I felt like an idiot. I went home that night and deleted the posts that I didn't want the world to read, and ever since that day, have remembered that whatever I write on the internet may well be seen by anyone. The words I publish on a blog or in a book can be read by my parents, my pastor, my landlord, my employer, my future children and grandchildren. It's with this awareness that I'm still determined to keep writing and to keep sharing my words.

I eventually transitioned to my blog www.lovethatbetsy.com. In 2011, I wanted to begin a community blog for women, so I talked four of my dearest friends into joining me. We were an established group of five girlfriends, already calling ourselves "The Cherokee Chix." Having scattered from our shared house on Cherokee Road in Tennessee, we kept in touch by email. I told these women, "You're all good writers! Let's start a blog together," so we did.

We shared a blog for five years, until our time was consumed with my book writing and them mothering houses full of children, so we shut down the blog. Even though I blogged regularly, I didn't feel like I was a real writer. I dreamed of becoming an author, and writing books one day.

Early in 2013, I was visiting family in North Carolina, and made a spontaneous decision to attend a workshop hosted by author and speaker Lynette Lewis. The seminar was intended to help women define and pursue their God-given dreams. One dream I identified that morning was my desire to write a book. My first step toward becoming an author was physically writing the words "to write a book" on my dream chart.

Six months later I made another last-minute decision, this time to attend a writers' conference hosted by my church. I entered the building that Friday night thinking "I want to be a writer." By the time the conference ended on Sunday, I had a deep understanding that I am a writer, and I am called by God to write.

My shift in perspective was fueled by conference speakers, including bestselling author Mark Batterson, who posed the question: "Are you called to write?"

"If you're called," he said, "Then you should write as an act of obedience to God. When I sit down at my keyboard, I don't type. I obey. I worship. I sometimes sacrifice." Stephen Roach, another speaker at this conference, expressed it like this: "When God gives us something to write, the writing becomes stewardship." As a Christian writer, I realize that I am a vessel, writing the message that God has put on my heart.

When I walked out the door of that conference with the gift of a quill pen in hand, I had a new, deep realization that I am an author. I knew that God wanted me to write about my experience of infertility and the insight He had given me along the way. I toyed with the idea of writing a novel that would describe the heart and the struggle of women in this situation. My idea of writing a novel didn't go far, because I knew that God was calling me to write my own story instead of fiction.

Writing, sharing about, and publishing *Embracing Hope During Infertility* was by far the most challenging thing I've done in my life so far. It was more difficult than obtaining a bachelor's degree, and requiring more details than planning our wedding for two hundred guests. I felt stressed, exhausted, and terrified, yet at the same time I felt so strongly called and determined to finish that book. It was as if I were pregnant with an idea; it was growing, it was going to come out, and I needed to birth this dream that God had placed inside of me. I chose to self-publish that book through

Amazon's platform CreateSpace, as well as creating an electronic Kindle version.

Friends and family surrounded my husband and me as we embarked on this journey of writing and publishing, and I could not have done it without their help. I knew very little about how to write or publish or market a book, so in a sense, *Write Your Story* is the guide I wish I'd had a few years ago. That's what people often do: they write the book they wish they could have read when they needed it. That's what happens when a person with a pioneer spirit holds a quill pen. (For the record, I don't write with a quill pen. It sits on my desk to remind me that I am a writer.)

In 2014, I began leading Unlocking Words, a writers' group hosted by my church. I correspond with writers, facilitate a monthly meeting, listen to others share their writing and their book ideas, read manuscripts, and encourage others to write. When I stepped into this role of leading a monthly meeting for writers, God pointed me toward Proverbs 20:5: "The purposes of a person's heart are deep waters, but one who has insight draws them out."

God reminded me that each writer attending our meetings came with a deep well of words that needed to be shared. It was my desire to obey the Holy Spirit by helping each person draw out what God had placed inside his or her heart.

There is a cartoon I've seen on the internet, where a patient is sitting on the doctor's exam table, and together the patient and doctor are discussing an x-ray that shows a book stuck inside the person's ribcage. The doctor says, "Good news! You've got a book in you, just waiting to come out!"

By helping other authors, I feel like I'm a doula, assisting with the birthing process. It's like I'm a doula for book babies. If your "x-ray" has proven that you have writing inside you that needs to come out, I want to help you give birth. Currently, I have a full-time job, I'm a full-time wife, and I'm writing my own books.

That's why I'm putting every spare minute into writing this one – in hopes that it will assist you as you birth the book that's inside you.

If you feel like you have a book in your heart, or if you feel like there is a deep well of something that God wants you to write and share, I'm here to help you get it out. As I sit down to write this book, I feel overwhelmed by the amount of information that I could share. This is not intended to be an exhaustive how-to manual, instead it's more like the scrawl of a trailblazer's map, defining the trail I'm on, and suggesting how to overcome certain hurdles you might face along the way. I'm offering tips to take you from the conception of your idea to the finished product. So, go ahead and *Write Your Story*.

Chapter 3: When You Have a Book Idea

Maybe you're one of these characters in this story of life:

• You're a stay-at-home mom to little ones, and you have an idea for a children's book that nobody has written yet, and you want to write it.

• God gives you vivid dreams in the night, and those dreams have inspired a story you want to publish.

• You've had an unusual life experience and you want to share your story in a memoir.

• You write hilarious yet insightful Facebook posts, and your friends are begging you to turn your stories into a book, but you don't know what steps to take next.

• You have begun writing a novel, and you want to finish it and share it with the world.

• You're writing a devotional or a Bible study curriculum, but you don't know how to get it into people's hands.

• You have a teacher's heart, and want to consolidate your thoughts into a book that you can easily distribute.

The above scenarios are based on conversations I've had with people in the past year, so I know that there are many soon-to-be authors out there who simply need a nudge.

You might think that your story is not interesting. You might think that your testimony is not dramatic or exciting. However, no matter what you feel, every story is worth sharing when God is the Author.

Although God gives us liberty to make decisions in this "story" of our lives, at the same time, Psalm 139:16 says, "…all the days ordained for me were written in Your book before one of them came to be." He truly is the Author of life. A message I keep hearing from other Christians is that we need to share our stories. I fully agree that we should.

Although many people dream of one day writing a book, it seems that very few follow through with writing and publishing their words. Never has becoming a published author been so achievable, yet it still requires effort. Traditional publishing houses remain competitive, but independent publishing is attainable. If you have considered writing a book, then why not start now?

Why should I write a book?

I'd like to respond to that question with my own: Are you called? Do you have a passion to put thoughts into written words?

I know it can be tricky to define calling. How do you know you're called to write? For me, it's similar to my unwavering knowledge that my husband Mike is the one I'm called to spend a lifetime with. Together he and I feel certain that we are supposed to live in the Washington, D.C. area right now, we would even say that we're called to live here. The sense of calling starts with a nudge and is enveloped in peace.

I've wanted to write books since childhood. I believe that it's part of God's calling for me personally. If you have a sense that God wants you to write, then I'm glad you're reading this book. If you don't feel a strong sense of calling, you just have a desire to write, then no worries, you can write books too.

At that life-changing writers' conference, best-selling author and Washington, D.C. pastor Mark Batterson gave the opening talk, and his message included the question "Has God called you to write?" He said that if God has called you, then you should write your book, without worrying about publication or contracts or money. Simply sit down and write. He said that he had set a deadline for himself, feeling determined to publish his first book by his 35th birthday.

I didn't realize that I was so directly following his footsteps, but a year after his talk, I was months away from my 35th birthday, and I told myself that if I couldn't have a baby by age 35, I would give birth to a book instead. My first book hit the press a month after that birthday. (It took longer than planned, and I learned the hard way that just like babies don't always come when you plan for them, books don't either.)

Writing might be a calling, but it is also a gift. Has anyone ever told you that you have a gift for writing? Maybe you just think of yourself as an average writer, but here's some news: a lot of people don't like to write. If you communicate well in writing, then it might be a gift God has given you.

For many, writing brings such joy. It's our happy place. It's a place where we can glorify God. My friend and author Suzanne K. Lee borrowed a line from Eric Liddell who said, "When I run, I feel His pleasure." She would say that when she writes, she feels God's pleasure. It's a means of communing with God, of worshipping Him.

Whether writing is a calling, a gift, worship, or just something you enjoy, regardless of your motive, you can ask the Holy Spirit to direct you. When I sit down for a longer writing session, as I did today, I ask God to give me clear thoughts and ideas, to put the pieces together. Other times I'm simply jotting down the thoughts and ideas that I feel like God is dropping into my mind. Sometimes I get home from church and say, "Wow, I got seven emails this morning!" Then I realize that they're all from me, notes to myself with concepts or ideas to include in a book or blog post.

Remember that God is the Author of the best-selling book of all time, the Bible. While you're not going to write anything equivalent to the Word of God, the same Holy Spirit that raised Christ from the dead, the same Holy Spirit that inspired all Scripture is the Holy Spirit who lives inside of you. Ask for His anointing and direction as you write, and remember that your words have the power to change people's lives.

Keep in mind that you're not just writing for your peers today; your writing has the power to impact many generations. I've heard several Christian speakers talk about the importance of writing your own story, your legacy, not just for today's audience, but for your grandchildren, your great-grandchildren, and generations yet to come. Psalms 102:18 says, "Let this be written for a future generation, that a people not yet created may praise the Lord!" Obviously, the writer was referring to his own writing, which was Scripture, but we can apply that same principle: let our writing point future generations toward God.

When a writer I knew passed away sooner than expected, I grieved not only because she was no longer on this earth, but because I thought of her as a great writer, and in my opinion, she wasn't done yet. Write as though your life is short. Write because you have a story and a legacy that might speak to people here and now, but it can also speak to people for generations yet to come.

Whether your book is fiction or nonfiction, targeting an audience of children or adults, and whether the content of your book is overtly Christian or not, I believe that there is power in telling your story. Don't be afraid to tell your story from the middle! You don't have to wait for a happy ending. I shared my story only part-way through our many-year wait for a baby, and it reached readers in a unique way because they knew I understood.

Tell your story in the style that God has given you. Fiction will include pieces of your own story. It will reflect the core of who you are. Revelation 12:11 says that we overcome the evil one by the blood of Jesus and with our testimony. I believe that the enemy of our souls loses power when we share our stories. When we write our stories, others can learn from our experiences. Readers find themselves saying "I am not alone in my situation." We connect with others as we share our experiences and insights. People will be encouraged. Others will grow in their faith. People can learn from the truth you share in your book. Somebody needs to read it, and you need to write it.

I find writing to be very therapeutic. Solidifying my thoughts on paper has helped me make it through some tough years. Many years of infertility, financial struggles, wrestling to believe that God is good even through difficult circumstances, overcoming fear of publicly sharing my testimony without a happy ending – writing and publishing throughout all of this has matured me, grown my faith in God, and weakened the enemy's power over my life.

As you ponder your story idea, whether it's fiction or non, for juveniles or adults, consider how your book will flow as a story. Some nonfiction books explain a process, like this one. I like it when nonfiction books still flow along, keeping the reader interested, and containing elements of story.

Writing is certainly an individual sport; it's something you must do on your own. The only person who will bring your book to life is you. However, it's important to build a support network of people to share ideas with and people to test-read or beta read your books. Get to know other authors so that you can exchange ideas and encourage each other. Finally, throughout your writing process, think about those who will read your book. They are your audience, and you need to connect with them before your book launch.

Perhaps you have a story or a message, but you don't think of yourself as a writer. Let me tell you something: you are a writer.

Repeat this out loud, no matter where you are right now:

I am a writer.

Did you say it? Now say it again.

I am a writer.

Repeat those words as many times as it takes for you to believe it. Write them down. If you have dream or calling to write, if you have the ability to write, then you are a writer, so start saying it—and believing it.

Chapter 4: Sit Down and Write

Finding the time to write is challenging. Right now, I am sitting at a table in a quiet corner of a library, where I will sort my thoughts and write them down until the library closes.

I have walked into the children's section of libraries and felt overwhelmed by the amount of options. I have stepped into the Christian bookstore and wondered if my book would ever make it onto those shelves. I have written blog posts wondering who will read my blog when there are so many out there. When God has given you the desire to write or create, then you should write or create.

This chapter title "Sit Down and Write" might sound overly simple, but it's harder than it might seem to intentionally sit down and write the words in your head. People who write often in a journal or on a computer might get a lot of words written, yet struggle to organize their words into a solid manuscript.

Many writing experts say that you should write your first draft by dumping all your words onto paper or the computer screen, without editing as you go. Once you've written a rough first draft, then you should go back and edit or rewrite your manuscript into something more workable.

I generally agree with this advice; however, I don't follow it. Maybe I'll do things differently in the future, but for my first few manuscripts I have collected everything I had previously written about the topic, such as blog posts about infertility or emails I'd written containing the information I need. Then I compile them into a document and begin to sort through them.

I liken writing to quilting. I have not attempted to sew a quilt, although my mother sews them beautifully. Writing can be like patchwork quilts made by pioneers traveling by wagon train. They saved bits and pieces of quality fabric, taking a piece of Grandpa's favorite shirt, a square of cloth from little sister's old baby outfit, a bit of lace from mom's wedding veil, and a shred of big brother's overalls. They would cut these pieces out, carefully arrange them, and stitch them together to create something beautiful. Despite all the different sources, the cloth is pieced together into a lovely arrangement.

I have been working on an upcoming book that involves stories of missionaries eating monkey soup, me being stranded in Africa at age 20, and lessons learned from hitting more than one deer at a high speed. When these different experiences are pieced together, together they demonstrate the goodness of God in all circumstances. While writing, I find myself quilting a book that I hope will interest and engage my readers.

How will you write?

Some people prefer to write on paper. Hats off to you; I don't like it. (Thanks, Mom, for requiring me to take that typing class in high school!) The extent to which I write on paper is in a couple of journals and on many loose scraps of paper. My notes to self are here, there, and everywhere, as Dr. Seuss might say. It makes me a messy writer, but as I collect those thoughts (or quilt pieces) and begin to patch them together, it works for me.

Maybe you're a linear thinker. Maybe you sit down and write a story from beginning to end. I've heard novelists describe the process of outlining a story before writing it. Others sit down and begin writing, not knowing what's coming until they start the next chapter. Some don't write the story in the order that you see in the finished copy. Others begin, then outline as they go.

When I write, I prefer to sit at a table with my laptop and let my fingers fly. I use a small, inexpensive, netbook-sized laptop.

(We're going to talk about publishing-related expenses later in this book.) My laptop is small and lightweight, making it easy for me to carry it back and forth to work every day. When I have a quiet moment during my day, I write. If I want to stop at the library on my way home from work, my writing tool is already in my bag. In fact, I'm sitting at the library right now because I find it to be less distracting and more inspiring than my house. (To my left I can look out a huge window at nature, and to the right I see endless rows of books. It's as if those who have pioneered before me in this journey of becoming an author cheer me on from the shelves.) Whether you're writing on paper then transferring to a computer, or writing from a desktop computer or laptop, find what you're comfortable with. Write in a place that is not distracting. Turn your back on that pile of laundry or dishes. Stay off the time-sucking internet, unless you really need to be there for research or communication. Sit down and write a real book instead of writing on Facebook.

Many established authors recommend using a writing software called Scrivener. (You can learn more about it at their website: www.literatureandlatte.com/scrivener.php.[1]) However, I always find myself coming back to Microsoft Word to write my books. Maybe I should be developing a better habit by writing in Scrivener, maybe not. I'm just glad to be writing.

I find Microsoft Word to be straightforward. It's the same program I've been using since I was writing papers in college nearly twenty years ago. The most recent updates are helpful, automatically highlighting spelling errors and phrasing that could be simplified.

If you do not have access to Microsoft Word or Scrivener, you can use Google docs or other basic writing software to begin your books. The bottom line is that you need to simply sit down and write. If you're not doing this, you're not going to finish your book.

Now Get Moving

"What? I just settled into my chair to write," you might wonder. Along with developing the habit of sitting down to write, I also suggest that you establish the habit of going outside for a walk or a run before or during a writing session. Other authors recommend this, and I've found it to be very beneficial. First, it's not good for our bodies to sit at a computer for hours on end. This can cause back pain, weight gain, and other health-related problems. When I sit at a table with my knees tucked under me, this causes knee pain later.

Walking or running also make a huge difference to my mind. I've run off and on for the past few years and many times as I finish up a run and begin a cool-down walk, writing ideas begin popping like popcorn in my mind.

I heard a writer talk about sitting on an exercise ball at the writing desk to stay fit while writing. This will strengthen your core and keep you alert. If you slouch, you'll fall off the ball.

If you're sitting in a chair at a table or desk, or anywhere else, be aware of your posture and your hand position. Poor positioning can quickly lead to headaches or back, wrist, and hand pain, and you will need all those parts to keep working well so that you can continue writing.

Maybe you need to take a break from sitting or walking to lie down for a moment. Did you know that different people get their best ideas in a variety of postural positions?

To write a book, you must be a self-starter and an independent worker. Although much of the writing and publishing process may be supported by the community of people surrounding you, it's entirely up to you to sit down and write that book, to follow through and finish, even when it's challenging.

Someone needs to hear your story. Your words might bring comfort to someone's pain, encouragement to those ready to give up, truth to deception, or simply the laugh that someone needs. The number one thing you must do in order to publish a book is sit down and write it. Unless you're co-authoring a project, writing is an individual activity. Starting and finishing your book is completely up to you. You'll need a support network, but you are responsible for putting your idea on paper and sharing your message with those who need to read it.

Remember that your words have creative power. They can be life-giving to others, and at times, your words will bypass the mind and speak to the spirit. That's how you can read a poorly written note, or an unpolished manuscript, and feel encouraged or refreshed. Someone needs to read your words. Will you sit down and write them?

Chapter 5: How?

We can face many hurdles as we write, ranging from the classic writer's block to wanting to give up to feeling jealous of the success of other authors. This chapter addresses some practical concerns and the next chapter focuses on spiritual and emotional struggles.

What if I'm feeling writer's block?

Writer's block is when a person sits down to write but they can't figure out where to begin or what to do. It's when a writer stares at a blank piece of paper or an empty computer screen, hoping for divine inspiration. Prayer is always a good place to begin, so ask God to give you ideas. Sometimes I start small, by writing a short social media post or a quick email. (Then I must log out of social media, because it will suck away valuable time.) Today as I sat down to work on this book, I searched for "write your story" in my email account to find the many, many emails that I had sent myself. That's what I tend to do, at work, at a stoplight, in bed, or in church, an idea pops into my head, and in my attempt to not lose it, I send myself a quick email.

I often listen to music while I write, although some people prefer silence. Others listen to gentle background noise, such as a white noise app. Do you play an instrument or like to sing? I play the guitar well enough to sing songs of worship to my Creator. Singing and playing an instrument stirs up my creativity while redirecting my heart toward God. Taking a break from writing to sing gives me a fresh energy for writing.

Sometimes I need to get my creative juices flowing, and other times I've overcome writers' block by getting out of my chair and going for a walk or a run to get my blood pumping and ideas flowing.

What if I simply do not have the time?

Guess what? I don't have time either. Currently I'm working on my third and fourth books, hoping to see each one in print as soon as possible. Writing books consumes my spare time, leaving me to wonder what people do on a Saturday when they're not working full time and writing on the weekends. However, I realize that I enjoy writing as my creative outlet, spending the time writing that other women might spend making crafts or redecorating their homes.

Sometimes I write at home, other times you might find me writing on my laptop in a waiting room, or at the library where I've stopped on my way home from work. All my books thus far have been written and published on my own during years of my life when my workday and commute takes well above eight hours each Monday through Friday.

I don't have the time to write, but I make the time. When the children I nanny are all at school and I have free time, I find a quiet place to write. I'm usually too tired to write before or after my work days, but when the inspiration hits, I sit at my computer when I come home from work. Most weekends I set aside some time for writing. When I have an extra day off work, such as a holiday or snow day, writing becomes a top priority. (Many authors have an additional source of income along with writing, which I will talk about later.)

Several years ago, I listened to the audiobook called *Eat That Frog! 21 Great Ways to Stop Procrastinating and Get More Done in Less Time* by Brian Tracy[1]. A quote from Mark Twain inspired the title. He said, "Eat a live frog first thing in the morning and nothing worse will happen to you the rest of the day."

The book suggests prioritizing your tasks with the most difficult first, and your day will get easier as it goes. If you "eat a frog" by being determined to fit writing time into the front end of your day, you'll make it happen. Or maybe other duties are the "frog" that you need to eat, such as cleaning your house, calling your insurance company, going to the gym (those are all tasks that I like to put off until later). If you knock those out and don't leave them hanging over your head, then you'll have time and freedom time to write.

At the Unlocking Words writers' conference, Stephen Roach shared practical wisdom about how to cultivate daily rhythms to bear fruit in our writing. He told us to journal regularly and dedicate time to write, not just when we feel like it. "Spontaneity should be the reward of preparation, not the result of disorganization," he said. He also pointed out that, "The key to discipline is desire." If you really want to write that book, you'll figure out how to discipline yourself to write it.

What if I don't know how to organize my writing into a book?

Consider asking a trusted friend or writing partner to sit down with you and help you sort out your writing. Ask God to help you as you begin to tackle this project. Like organizing a messy part of your home, you simply must sort piece by piece, putting it into proper order. As a creative person, it's not just going to be in order, but it will also be a work of art.

What about busy moms?

I love learning about how moms write books, maybe because being a wife/mom/author is my dream career (and I am currently expecting my first baby). As a thirty-something woman, I realize that many women in my peer group are mothers of young children. Some wish they could write, but simply don't feel like they have the time or energy. I suggest that you prayerfully consider whether or not God wants you to work on your book right now.

If God is prompting you to focus on your family or something else, then you can pursue your writing later. But if you're hearing His whisper that now is the time to begin writing, here are some nuggets of wisdom I've picked up from moms who write.

I've heard a couple of mom authors say that they write when their children are in school. One writes six hours a day from her home office while her children are at school. Another shared that she goes to a coffee shop and writes during school hours, which allows her to focus on mothering when her children are home.

Homeschooling mamas might be wondering when they can fit writing into their schedule. I heard author Elizabeth Maddrey speak at a conference and wondered how she finds the time to write so many books. She says she sits down to write most evenings after she puts her children to bed. They have a routine: kids go to bed and she writes. When I've been an overnight nanny for a week at a time, I don't have any energy or creativity left after the children finally fall asleep. I've wondered if there are other blocks of time homeschooling moms can find. My friend and author Cathy Harris also homeschools her children. She shared with me that she typically focuses on writing for a couple of hours each afternoon. The school day is finished, and her children are either napping, reading, or playing. She is available if they need her, but this routine allows her time to write.

I've heard it said that we shouldn't do projects in our time alone that we can do when our children are around. For example, if you need focused, quiet, writing time, zone in on that when you're alone. Save the lighter, easier projects for when children are in the room, and more likely to interrupt you.

Could you find quiet time to write while your children nap? How about waking up extra early a few days a week for several weeks or months to finish your book? Would your husband be able to give you three hours on Saturday to go to a library to write all alone?

Experiment, and find what works for you, if writing is your focus at this point in your life. Maybe you need to concentrate on caring for your children or your home. Maybe holding down a job and raising a family is all that you can manage right now. That's okay! You might need to put your book idea on the back burner, but if the book is burning inside of you, ready to come out, then ask God to make a way.

A fun book to read through is *Daily Rituals: How Artists Work* by Mason Currey[2]. This book chronicles how famous artists and authors produced their work, describing their sleeping and eating and drinking habits. Some write with coffee or tea, and some authors apparently write proficiently while drinking alcohol. It's fascinating to know what works for other people: some people get up early in the morning to write before their work day, others work late into the night. Some find their groove in the middle of the day. Some writers sit at a table, others lie on the couch. You should discover your best times and places for writing.

What additional suggestions would I give an aspiring author?

Read the Bible

Christian authors need to saturate their minds with the Word of God. Try listening to an audio Bible as well as reading it. Memorize Scripture and write it down. Pray it out loud. Not only will these things affect you spiritually, there are no better words for Christian authors to meditate on than the Word.

Read Frequently

Make sure you're spending more time reading books and less time reading Facebook or other social media posts. Turn off the television, or limit yourself. I'm thankful for parents who encouraged a love for reading books and magazines. As a child, I read my way through the children's section of the library in elementary school and I haven't stopped reading since then. Several years ago, I began using the website and app called Goodreads[3] to track the books that I read. This discipline challenges me to read even more. I read a variety of fiction and non, some best sellers and some poorly edited self-published works. I read juvenile fiction, and I read books on similar topics to what I'm writing about. Each of these things has helped me to become a better writer.

Through reading a person can subconsciously understand the flow of how a book should go, taking note of the layout, improving one's spelling and grammatical skills. By reading we become better writers. Use a Kindle and read on the go. Use it while exercising on a treadmill or elliptical machine at the gym. I read e-books on airplanes, while waiting in line, or in the dark, before I go to sleep. With my e-reader, I can borrow digital audio books from the library and listen to them while I drive, clean the house, or exercise.

Children first learning to read will become better spellers and writers after practicing reading. Likewise, spending time with books helps adults write better as well.

Write Abundantly

My first completed book manuscript held over 40,000 words, although many more words did not make it into the final copy of the book. (I'm so impressed when novelists crank out an 80,000-word story!) After blogging for several years, I realized that only about half of the posts I write ever make it onto the blog. I simply don't like them enough or feel like they're finished enough. Some words are still sitting in the computer document or bouncing around in my head, waiting for the right time to be shared. I'm not sure that I want to make everything I write public. And some posts simply need to be rewritten to become good enough to hit the web. By writing more than what you ever share with others, you will be able to share only the very best of your work.

Published writing should be well written. There are plenty of manuals and resources to improve your writing, so I'm not going to focus on that here. Later I will talk about the importance of editing, so I want to assure you that even if you know that your spelling or grammar need improvement, a good editor can clean those up for you. Please make sure that your writing is professional when you publish it. Readers like me will catch your spelling and grammatical errors (and if you catch mine, please let me know).

Connect with Other Writers

We have endless opportunities to network with other authors via the internet. Follow other writers on social media. Search for author groups on Facebook by genre. I'm part of several Facebook groups (Christian, indie, children's books) where I glean ideas from others. Join an organization focused on your genre, such as American Christian Fiction Writers[4]. Join a local writers' group. (Look online or inquire at your library. If you live in the Washington, D.C. area I attend two Christian writers' groups there.) Comment on your favorite authors' posts and get on their radars. Go to book signing events and meet other authors.

Support other authors by reading, reviewing, and sharing about their books. I put forth effort to do these things, especially for a first-time author. I know how much other people's support means to me when I launch a book, and I want to support others as well. Although it might feel like it at times, writing and publishing is not a competition. Christian authors should be cheering each other on.

Learn about Writing and Publishing

I know several people who pursued master's degrees in writing. Although going back to school is not my current plan, I attend every writers' workshop that I'm able to attend. I have not regretted this; every single one has exceeded my expectations because there is so much to learn in this ever-changing world of technology. I glean so much wisdom and insight from other authors. I also read books on writing and listen to audiobooks.

Despite the storylines I do not care for, I found Stephen King's audiobook *On Writing A Memoir of the Craft*[5] very interesting and inspiring. The resources section at the end of this book will list books, podcasts, and networking opportunities to consider.

Stay Humble

I may not be the best author, yet I'm a determined one. I'm actively writing books that I would want to read. I feel happy when I feel like a successful author. Yet I remind myself that writing books is not a competition (and I am competitive by nature). I don't have to be the best. I don't have to be a best seller. It's tough in the age of social media "likes" and "followers," because it's so easy to compare ourselves via the internet. As Christian writers, we should be glorifying God above all else. We should be building each other up, not fighting to get to the top. While I was writing this book, a speaker at a conference I attended focused on the scripture Philippians 2:3, "Do nothing out of selfish ambition or vain conceit. Rather, in humility value others above yourselves..." Remember that scripture as a writer in the social media generation. It's not all about me or the words I write or the stories I tell. Our Christian principles should determine our choices as writers.

Publish from a Place of Healing

How do we write about hurtful or negative situations, especially from a Christian perspective? My first suggestion is that you cover your writing in prayer, asking God to direct you in your unique situation.

Writing can be therapeutic. Pouring my feelings into words and making sense of my experiences through writing helped me survive and sometimes even thrive through years of waiting for motherhood. I often say that writing is my free therapy. Journaling or writing can be a safe place to process the good and the bad. However, how much of the bad stuff do we post on our blog or publish in our books?

I was privileged to hear author Anna Whiston-Donaldson, author of *Rare Bird: A Memoir of Loss and Love*[6], give a talk about grief. As a mom and blogger, her grief became public when her twelve-year-old son died suddenly in a tragic accident. Not long after, she was offered a book contract to write her story. She shared with us that her first draft was full of anger, and she asked the publisher for an extension while she continued to sort through her feelings. Her memoir, published three years after Jack's death, feels raw and real, as if the reader is walking alongside Anna as she grieves, yet it does not leave the reader feeling angry or bitter. I have read other memoirs that make me feel yucky and bogged down by the trauma the writer has experienced. There is an element of emotion that is important to include when writing a memoir, However, Christian authors need to think about how our reader will feel. Do you want your reader to walk away being drawn closer to God, feeling hope and encouragement? Do you want them to feel as awful as you did during your hardship?

What if the topic of our writing is someone who has hurt or offended us? I think it's important to treat others with honor, even when they've wronged us. We don't want to ignore the bad stuff, sweeping it under a rug. However, it might not be your place to air someone else's dirty laundry. Take it too far, and you might face a lawsuit for defamation.

One way to handle this is to keep the negativity to a minimum. Yes, you can describe the offense or the hurt or the abuse, but how about limiting it to just a few paragraphs while focusing the bulk of your story on the redemption? (This is specifically for those writing nonfiction.)

Another idea is to change the name and scenario enough that the offending person wouldn't even recognize himself in your story. This way you can still communicate the difficulty with your reader, who might need to hear about how you overcame your pain, but not slander the person who hurt you.

Dumping your feelings into words on a page might be exactly what you need to do as you wrestle through your pain, grief, or offense. But that first draft might not be what others need to read. Let your writing be part of your healing, then let the words you publish benefit other people's healing. I see tremendous benefit in getting free from the baggage that life and other people bring, whether that is through counseling or prayer times with others. Your writing can reflect your pain, but I believe it will bring greater hope and healing to others if you are also hope-filled and healed. Write freely, but publish wisely.

Chapter 6: These Struggles are Real

You have an idea for a book, you sense God calling you to write, and you know that you need to simply sit down and do it. Take a moment to address some of the spiritual opposition and emotional struggles that you might experience. Each of these might be a writer's block to overcome. I have wrestled with these, and while listening to other authors, I realize that these issues are common.

I know that the enemy of our souls wants us to be like a clogged up well, not springing forth like the deep waters described in Proverbs 20:5. The enemy wants to silence our testimony; he doesn't want anyone to gain hope or encouragement from our stories of faith and truth. The devil will use some nasty tricks to knock us down and shut us up.

Even though I love writing books, I've faced many emotional and spiritual hurdles along the way. As a new author, I want you to know that you might face these issues, and if you do, here are some suggestions for how to fight them. I hope you don't wrestle with any of these to the degree that I have, but fear, failure, rejection, disappointment, jealousy, depression and wanting to quit are all feelings that I have experienced throughout the process of publishing two books. I've wrestled against a fear of "what will people think?" even as I write this. These are all ugly monsters that want to silence my voice, but I know I am called by God to write and to cheer you on as well.

Fear

The summer after I turned 19, I lived in Panama, Central America, serving as a short-term missionary with a ministry called

Youth With A Mission. I was invited to join another teen missions group for a one week outreach in the Darien jungle. One morning as I woke up under my mosquito net in the large hut we used for sleeping quarters, I heard the other girls on the team whispering to each other: "Where have all the guys gone?"

Looking around confirmed that early in the morning, all the males from our team had left. We soon discovered that they had gone hunting with the local men. Sure enough, a couple of hours later the village men and the American teen boys returned with their catch. Hanging from a pole suspended between shoulders were a cute little dead monkey and a more unusual small animal they called a jungle cat. Curiously, I followed the crowd toward a kitchen hut, and watched as they began to skin the monkey. My stomach could only handle so much, so I left midway through the preparation.

"They're going to eat that monkey," the teenagers whispered to each other.

Then a greater fear was realized.

"Oh no, they're going to feed us that monkey!"

That evening, our group heaved a corporate sigh of relief when monkey did not appear on our dinner plates, and we were given tuna fish sandwiches for dinner. Suddenly tuna fish, a food I had never enjoyed, sounded very appealing. I was glad to know that the locals would eat their chunky monkey soup and we could eat our tuna.

However, the next day, when it was time for our noon meal, the local villagers brought a meal to our hut. We watched in dread as they carried a huge pot of soup. Monkey soup.

I wasn't eager to taste it, but we were obligated to eat whatever was set before us, out of respect for the culture we were in. Remembering this requirement, our group of western teenagers tried our best to consume our meal as to not offend those who had offered it to us.

"What did monkey taste like?" People have asked when I've shared this story.

"I have no idea," I reply. "I dumped salt into that soup and tried to swallow it, then discreetly tried to throw away as much as possible."

Years later, as I turned 35, I published *Embracing Hope During Infertility*. Writing about our struggle to start our family was therapeutic, yet sharing what I wrote with others was terrifying. Publishing this book was my greatest step of vulnerability at that point in my life. I wrote about my struggle to become a mother, baring my soul, disclosing my medical history, and then making it available for anyone in the world to read it.

I felt like I was sharing my personal diary on Amazon.

Many months before publishing, I shared the idea of the book with my husband, then with my sister and my closest friends. I began telling my parents, my in-laws, and eventually I shared it on social media. I was nervous about sharing such a personal subject.

Questions harassed my thoughts. I asked myself things like: What if I'm not a good writer? What if nobody wants to read it? What if people hate it? What if I write about my faith that God will provide us children one day, and what if I never have children?

Fear haunted me regularly.

It was through that process that I learned something about taking a huge step to overcome a challenge or a fear. When recounting my monkey soup story to a friend around the time I published that book, I told her that after eating monkey soup I have been able to at least try any food, even if I really didn't like it.

Every other food that has been placed before me since that adventure in Panama seems easy to eat by comparison.

She commented that publishing my first book on a topic as personal as my own infertility story was like eating monkey soup, because everything else would feel easier in comparison. After seeing a freshly-skinned monkey and tasting its meat, unusual foods don't stress me out like they once did. After vulnerably sharing my most difficult and intimate struggles, I embraced my God-given calling as a writer with more boldness than before.

Not only do I wrestle with the fear of sharing my writing, but I wrestle with fear about promoting my books. I worry that I am getting on people's nerves when talking about what I've written. I fear rejection.

When you trust the Lord to take a step of overcoming fear, especially when you become vulnerable out of obedience to God, you will find that you fear less. Maybe you're not completely fearless in all things, but without a doubt, there will be less fear.

Remember that you are writing out of obedience and calling and that God will give you the strength to face your fears.

Failure

Are you really wrestling with failure, or with fear of failure? I think that fear of failure is a tremendous struggle for creative people. We worry about failing, and if something is not an immediate success, we might think that we have failed. I enjoy watching the movie *Eddie the Eagle*, about a young man determined to compete in the Olympics, although he seemed to lack all athletic ability. His story of perseverance beyond failure inspires me. It's like Thomas Edison's said, "I have not failed, I've just found 10,000 ways that won't work."

So, what if I've written a book that hasn't sold well? I can write another book or figure out how to sell the first one. As an author, you have the opportunity to write and create for the rest of your life. Your writing career doesn't have to end until you take your last breath.

Writing is a process. I've written books and published them. Maybe I haven't sold as many copies as I would like, but does that make me a failure? I've received an Amazon review that simply says "Hated it." Does that mean I'm a failure?

Trusting God as an author involves believing that God isn't calling me a failure. If my book doesn't sell a single copy, or if my book isn't as "successful" as I might wish, that doesn't mean I'm a failure. It might mean that I have room to grow. It might mean that God simply wanted me to obey His call. It doesn't mean that I should stop writing.

One Sunday morning our church enjoyed hearing a spontaneous song that was sung to the artists in our church. The young man sang prophetic encouragement to us, and one phrase that he sang went like this: "You are as creative as you were created to be."

God made us in His own image and He is the Creator of all. He has already deposited creativity into us. We simply need to write it down, or paint it, or dance it, or sing it, or play it.

Remember that your Creator has made you Creative, so be bold and release what He has put inside of you. He's the One who drowns our fear of failure in His perfect love, so that we can simply be who He's created us to be.

Rejection

As a writer, it's likely that you will deal with feelings of rejection. Ask just about any author who has published with a large publishing house, and it's likely that their writing was turned down by others before landing a deal. Traditional publishing is a competitive marketplace. Independent publishing also feels competitive, but in a different way. I'll describe this further in Chapter 10.

Back in the days when we saved documents on floppy disks, I followed standard procedure and submitted an article to a Christian publication by mailing the document on a disk, enclosing my cover letter. The editor's response came a few weeks later. Her rejection letter was politely phrased, but I felt discouraged because she turned my piece down. I didn't tell a soul, but I did let feelings of rejection eat away at my own soul, thus bogging down my writing dreams for years to come.

I thought that my one submission was good enough. When it wasn't, I assumed that nothing I ever wrote would be good enough. I still dreamed of becoming an author, but my dream was tucked deep down into my soul, where a monster named rejection also remained.

Ask any published writer if their writing has been rejected by a publication, and the answer is likely "yes." Most manuscripts are rejected by publishing houses, some repeatedly. It's not unusual for articles to be declined by publications. Most of my attempts at guest posting for other blogs have been rejected. Only one person can win a writing contest at a time. Does that mean that we should give up?

Feelings of rejection are not limited to when a writer is trying to get published. Since becoming a published author, I applied to participate in a leadership role at a conference. It felt like a long shot, but I wanted this opportunity. I was turned down, while some peers were chosen. Overwhelming feelings of rejection hit me hard, once again. When I watch someone else get a writing or speaking opportunity that I hope for, I feel rejected, and I feel jealous (which I will talk about soon, so keep reading).

Rejection is not a reason to quit writing. Instead it is part of the process of becoming a writer. Let each incident of rejection prompt you to find another way to share your story or to share it better. It can inspire your creativity instead of bogging you down.

Disappointment

This is my least favorite topic to discuss, probably because it still feels raw some days. I hope to spare you from the pit of disappointment. (If you're reading this chapter and feeling your emotions stirred up by any of these topics, please go to God in prayer and ask Him to help you sort through your feelings and deal with your sinful nature, and ask Him to direct your steps.)

I think many writers publish their first book with an expectation that it will take off and soar. All we must do is write a book, and people will buy it, right? Unfortunately, it's typically not that easy.

We might expect others to support our books by buying copies, selling it in their bookstore, or by promoting it to help us out. However, it's not easy to get people to buy a book, and even if everyone in your immediate circle of friends and family buys a copy, it might be tough to promote sales beyond your immediate sphere of influence.

It's easy to feel disappointed. A person you thought would promote it doesn't even buy a copy. A church you hoped would help spread the news remained silent. The people you asked to write a review of your new book didn't. After publishing my first book, someone invited me to come speak to a group about having hope during infertility. Several times I tried to follow up to set a date, and the person never responded to my emails. That is one example, but several times other Christians, friends who had experienced infertility, and people who I thought would help me with opportunities to share about my book were far from supportive.

Events like this made me think, "Well, if people I know won't support my book, then how will I ever convince strangers to read it?" As a new author trying to figure out how to spread the word about a book, it's very easy to get bogged down by disappointment.

If your book isn't earning money or your sales rank low on Amazon, you might feel disappointed. The friends and family who said, "That's great, you wrote a book!" never bought a copy. Your feelings of disappointment can make you want to quit, and they can make you feel angry toward others. Neither are good solutions. Go before God in prayer. Tell Him you feel disappointed. Ask Him for direction with your book. And redirect your own perspective, reminding yourself that all you need to do is to be faithful in the little things. Do you believe that God put this book on your heart? Do you feel that He directed you to write it? If so, then you've been obedient to Him, which is your number one priority.

I suspect that most people do not realize how much effort goes into the writing and publishing of a book. Others may not realize how desperately we want to be supported in our endeavors. We cannot hold anyone else to an unrealistic expectation of what others should do for us. Instead, we should be grateful for all who help us out as authors, and we should remember to encourage, endorse, and cheer on other authors.

Ultimately, when fighting disappointment, we must be obedient to the direction God has set before us, being faithful to the things He has called us to do, instead of focusing on the support of other people.

Jealousy

I see the green-eyed monster of jealousy in young children, and it's not pleasant. Not only is it unpleasant, it's often ridiculous. Being upset because another sibling got to eat a cupcake at a birthday party at school seems just plain silly.

Then I became an author, and my competitive nature resurfaced. My desire to be chosen, to be first and best has caused me to envy other authors who seem to be more successful than me.

While sharing some of these feelings with a wise friend, she commented that my feelings of both rejection and jealousy are rooted in the lie that there is not enough. When I was unable to conceive a baby, I felt jealous when others have babies. That thought was based on the ridiculous lie that God does not have enough babies for everyone. It's like I'm thinking that my siblings have had all the babies and our parents are now maxed out on grandchildren, so no babies for me. What a ridiculous thought!

The same applies to writers: my peer was selected to help lead at a conference and I was not, another author was given an opportunity that I had hoped for, another independently published author reached a sales goal before I did. Each of these things has made me feel jealous, so you know what my friend reminded me? There are enough babies for all of us. There is enough space for everyone to write a book. There is enough, so I need not be jealous when another author achieves something I desire.

In recent months, as I have wrestled with my identity and calling as an author, I have realized that all I need to do is walk down the path God has called me to. He prompted me to write this book, so I'm doing it, not knowing how well it will be received.

Remember that conference speaking position I wasn't offered and I felt disappointed about? It was God's doing, because He didn't want me there. Days after receiving a rejection letter, God gave me the one and only free ticket to an indie-publishing conference, confirming that this is the route He's placed me on. God confirmed that He knows what He's doing by closing doors to some speaking opportunities I had dreamed of, then giving me remarkable peace about the speaking engagements He has dropped in my lap. Focusing on what God has called me to, not what others are doing, helps me to conquer jealousy.

Depression

I haven't been clinically diagnosed with depression, although I experience some depressed feelings at times (especially in the dark, cold winter). Sometimes the process of writing and publishing a book feels very much like a pregnancy and a birth. With my first book, I felt so strongly that I needed to "get this book out of me!" It was very emotional to give birth to it. Many other writers compare the birthing of books to the birthing of children. A friend who recently published her first book assured me that the book birthing process is much harder than delivering a baby, and she has three children!

I remember the desperate feeling I had with my first book: "I just need to be done with this!" I've seen enough Facebook posts about "I'm so ready to have this baby" that I know pregnant women often feel the same way. I remember the giddiness and exhaustion I felt on the day my book came into this world. However, I was not prepared for the emotional letdown that would follow.

I was already dealing with the discouragement of infertility, followed by disappointments after publishing my first book. People who I thought would help support me in practical ways simply said "congrats" and moved on with their lives, leaving me with this newborn book that I had no idea what to do with. Maybe I expected exhilaration after my first publication, but instead I found myself feeling rather blue, and very aware of all the work still before me.

Reasons we could feel depressed after publishing include the pressure that after you write a book, you want to sell it. You discover that you've got to market it. You've got to convince readers to read it, and encourage them to help you spread the word. Disappointment can get you down. Jealousy can whisper in your ear. Suddenly, you're an author, but you're also fighting battles you didn't know you would have to fight.

Dealing with these other struggles, these monsters of jealousy and disappointment and fear, will help new authors fight off the feelings of depression. From my own experience and from observing other authors, I assure you that if publishing a book is harder than you anticipated, you are not alone. Becoming an author has unique challenges, so remember your calling, remember why you're sharing your writing, and let your "why" be what keeps you going.

Unresolved Issues

It's possible that your writers' block can be related to unresolved conflict with other people. Are you writing the scene of a novel that mirrors a struggle you're having with a friend or family member? Maybe you feel stuck in your writing, but the root of the blockage is that you need to repent or make things right with another person. Sometimes the other party refuses to communicate, in that case do what you can to seek restoration of the relationship and get your heart right before God.

If you're writing nonfiction, especially something like a memoir, it's likely that there are people in your life who contributed to your story in a negative way, whether by abusing you or even unintentionally hurting you. Cover that writing with prayer, and ask God for direction. Share your story in a way that still honors the other person.

Suggestions I've heard from fellow Christian writers include changing the names, places, and situation enough that the person you are writing about wouldn't even recognize themselves in your story. Also, consider writing just enough about the negative situation to give a background so that the bulk of your writing can point people to God, remembering that He is the Redeemer and Healer.

If conflict with another person is holding you back from freely writing your story, get things right before God, and do your best to seek restoration with others. You might find that it unblocks your flow of words.

Wanting to Quit

I'm also learning that sometimes, as creative people, we draw or write, but we don't always finish our projects. The fastest way to fail at writing a book is to simply quit. It can be difficult to follow through. There may be situations where we know we should let go and move on from a project, but is this project one you feel that you should finish? Then you need to finish it.

This book has been difficult for me to finish, as life circumstances keep pushing it back. I'm determined to finish, and I'm determined to follow these tips that I write here.

I have never finished writing and publishing a book as quickly as I would have liked. One thing that slowed me down while writing this one was discovering I was pregnant (after seven years of asking God for a baby). The first trimester sapped me of energy. I've often compared writing and publishing a book to being pregnant and giving birth, and a fresh analogy that just came to my mind is that you can't stay pregnant forever. If God has placed a book idea on your heart that He is calling you to birth, or if you strongly feel that you need to write a certain book, don't wait unnecessarily. If you are pregnant with an idea, there will come a day when your book needs to be born, whether it's quickly with a few weeks gestation like an opossum, or whether the pregnancy takes nearly a couple of years like an elephant. (Let's face it, the gestational period of some books will be longer than an elephant's pregnancy of twenty-two months, but my point is, eventually give birth to your book. Don't stay pregnant with an idea forever.)

A children's book called *What Do You Do With an Idea?* by Kobi Yamada[1] uses vivid imagery to address some of these struggles we face as writers. Find a copy and encourage yourself by reading it. Also, the last time I picked it up I noticed that it is independently published and a *New York Times* best seller. It can be done!

When it comes to finishing a writing project, it's easy to simply drag our feet, allowing a project to be pushed aside and never returning to it, even if it's something we believed God was telling us to do in the first place. I've been reflecting on a characteristic of God: He finishes what He starts. Philippians 1:6 reminds us that "He who began a good work in you will carry it on to completion…" I remember singing "He who began a good work in you will be faithful to complete it," in church as a child, and it's true: God faithfully completes what He begins.

As an imitator of Christ, I want to create, and I want to finish.

Chapter 7: Editing

A woman in my writers' group lovingly confronted me just the other day. "Is our writer's group supposed to be just a place of encouragement, or are we supposed to be critiquing each other?" she asked me.

"Yes, we should be critiquing," I responded. "But it can be so scary! I don't want people to be afraid to share their writing."

If we don't receive ample and thorough feedback on our writing prior to publication, I believe that we will publish subpar writing. Our books or blog posts will not be excellent without editing. Yes, the editing process can be intimidating. Welcoming criticism of something you've poured your heart and soul into is tough. I've been there. In fact, I'm there right now as I write this book and seek input from other published writers and aspiring authors. Creative writing is the fun part, while seeking the opinion of others feels intimidating. Sometimes I still struggle with anxiety when I receive edits in my inbox, however after reviewing feedback, I'm always grateful for the insight of others.

To make our writing the best it can be, I highly encourage you to edit your work several times, and invite others to do so. My husband is an excellent editor; over the years he has assisted me by reading through most of my blog posts to catch grammatical errors. While writing my first book, I shared the manuscript with close to 20 people for proofreading. I needed to receive their input on my content, tone, grammar, and spelling. Editing is necessary for all writers.

Prior to publishing, blog posts and books should be cleaned up from obvious grammatical or spelling mistakes. Blog posts can be edited more freely, while books in print will flaunt their mistakes for years to come. Using a program such as Microsoft Word will help you to catch your spelling errors. Writers should regularly read high quality writing to develop an eye for excellent grammar and word usage.

Types of Edits

I once attended a very informative workshop led by freelance editor Bethany Kaczmarek. She broke down the editing process into these five categories, and gave me permission to share them here:

Macro/substantive edits involve working on the book's overall development, content, big picture ideas, and a general overview. Macro edits involve reading through your entire manuscript, not focusing on the spelling or punctuation, but helping your entire book flow from beginning to end. This is important to me as a reader: if a book doesn't flow smoothly and keep my interest, it's likely that I will set it aside and never finish it. As a writer, I want people to read my books, so having a macro edit will benefit me greatly.

Copy editing means fixing typos, rethinking word choices, correcting spelling, suggesting edits to paragraphing, as well as removing overused phrases and clichés. A copy editor will catch mistakes, and will let you know what phrases you've repeated too often or when your work sounds cliché. This type of edit tremendously helped my first book to succeed. A sub-category of copy editing would be a **mechanical edit**, where an editor would focus on spelling, punctuation and grammar.

A line edit is when an editor works through a manuscript line by line, making the work stand out. Line editors take your voice and your writing to the next level. In her workshop, Bethany shared, "A line editor makes your words sing, and a skilled line editor makes a good writer sound like a gifted writer."

Critique means the editor reads the entire manuscript without pausing to edit, then she makes suggestions of what to work on. A critique would be a less costly edit, but also less detailed. The editor would read it then give you general feedback, such as telling you that you need to work on punctuation, passive writing, or your descriptions.

Mentoring involves a lot of back and forth discussion throughout the process. Mentoring is just as it sounds: it involves someone walking through the entire manuscript with you.

One more area to consider as a Christian author, is having other Christians offer feedback prior to publishing. I realize that various Christian denominations hold differing opinions on theology, however I need a trusted reader to let me know if my words are going against God's Word.

Everyone should consider hiring a professional editor. Other authors consistently tell me how grateful they were for the remarks they received from an editor.

Counting the Cost

Hiring a professional editor requires finances. Costs can range from $250 – $3,000 to edit one full-length book. I realize that not all up-and-coming authors have that much available in their budget, especially if you're considering writing multiple books. Further resources and price lists can be found on the Editorial Freelancers Association[1] website www.the-efa.org.

When I wrote my first book, our finances were tight. Not knowing much about the process, I timidly began my editing process by asking friends and family members to proofread my manuscript to give me feedback. I didn't know what I was doing. I began by asking seven peers to proofread. Some simply read it then responded with "good job" or "you made me cry." Some provided an in-depth edit. Some suggested macro edits, like rearranging sections. Some caught theological or spelling errors.

Seven proofreaders turned into about twenty readers giving me the gift of an edit. Desiring one more review by someone who did not know me well, I asked an acquaintance for a final edit, and we paid her a small fee.

Before publishing your book, it will need to be edited by someone other than you. Even if you choose a less costly avenue, your book needs editing. Your raw writing and your ability to catch your own errors is not enough.

Considering Other Options

What if you're a new author on a tight budget and paying an editor is not a practical option? Although those who firmly believe in hiring an editor for each book may disagree with me, here are some alternative choices to consider.

Do you have friends or family members who are skilled editors, but are not currently working in that field? For example, I went to a small liberal arts college, and many of us graduated with a degree that sounded good, but wasn't practical for entering the workforce. Soon after graduating we discovered that having a degree in English or Biblical Studies didn't ensure a smooth transition into a job. Thankfully, several of my friends with English degrees helped me with *Embracing Hope During Infertility*. I still feel tremendous gratitude for their help.

I want to remind you that nobody wants to feel used, especially in the field where they work professionally. Typically, you don't ask a hairstylist to cut your hair for free if that is her means of income. If she offers her services for free, then receive it, but you cannot assume that a childcare provider wants to babysit for free, or that a professional photographer wants to take your pictures for free. Do not ask a professional editor to work on your book for free. However, if a trusted person in your life has the skill and is willing to help you edit your book because they believe in you or because they enjoy editing, then consider that option.

Are you part of a writers' community? Is there another author that you could trade services with – each of you could edit the other person's books? Editing takes time, but by trading services, you can save money. If you want a fair trade, then find someone whose skills match yours.

Beta Readers

Whether or not you hire a professional editor, it's important to use beta readers. A beta reader is not a professional editor, but it's a person who will read your book prior to publication to provide feedback.

This morning I excitedly read aloud my list of beta readers to my husband. I have found a dozen people who have expressed interest in reading *Write Your Story*. Once my draft is complete, I will email the document to my beta readers, and they will let me know their thoughts. Does it flow well? Does it hold your interest? Is the information helpful? What am I lacking? What errors have you found in my manuscript?

Although I did not know the term "beta reader" while preparing my first book (I didn't know much about publishing at all), my twenty-some friends and family who read and shared feedback with me were beta readers. Their responses were vital, with suggestions such as: "remain consistent with your punctuation," "tone down your opinion there or you'll turn people off" and "how about if you move this story to this other chapter?" Beta readers can also help you out when you release your book. They can talk about it on social media, write a review on Amazon, and encourage you when you need it.

Receive Feedback Prior to Publication

If you don't welcome some readers' feedback prior to publication, you will become aware of it after publishing. People will verbally tell you what they think of your book (and point out the errors they find), or responses will come by lack of sales, support, or enthusiasm. If you want to produce a book that is reader-friendly and that impacts people, then you must welcome criticism throughout the process.

Even though I've been growing as a writer since childhood, I often still feel insecure about sharing my writing. I don't feel like a professional, although I write regularly and my mind is overflowing with ideas of books to write and publish. The other day I heard someone quote Richard Bach: "A professional writer is an amateur who didn't quit." If you're feeling insecure, thinking that you're not educated enough or creative enough, remember that perseverance is key to becoming a published author.

You should keep writing, and be willing to receive feedback and critique from others. Author Elizabeth Maddrey said that she has learned more about writing from the editing process than she ever learned from books on writing. I feel the same way.

I recommend that we seek editing that will help us to maintain our own voice as the writer and help our writing flow more smoothly. We need others to correct our errors prior to publication.

Eventually Stop Editing

At some point, you've got to call it quits. You can refine your work more and more, but eventually you need to stop editing and call it done. Lauren Graham writes in her memoir *Talking as Fast as I Can: From Gilmore Girls to Gilmore Girls (and Everything in Between)* [2], "At some point you have to let it go, or it isn't a book for sale, it's a pile of papers on your desk."

Cover your work in prayer, receive feedback from others, and especially if you have perfectionist tendencies, let go and let your book go out into the world to do what it's intended to do.

Things to Remember

Thankfully there are many handbooks and online resources to help us write with excellence. Here are a few things to remember, especially if you decide to self-publish your book.

Citations: If you quote another person's writing, including song lyrics, you need to properly cite it. If you're quoting what someone else has said, make sure you ask permission. You don't want to plagiarize someone else's work or share a story that is not yours. If you cite Scripture, make sure your reader knows which version of the Bible you used. You can see an example of this in the copyright page of this book. The copyright page of a Bible outlines how to cite it. If you quote multiple versions of the Bible, reference each one properly.

Copyright Page: When I published my first book, I studied the copyright page of traditionally as well as independently published books in order to write my own. This page should include your ISBN as well as an "all rights reserved" blurb and the location or country of publication. You can register your copyright in the United States at www.copyright.gov[3].

Images: When using an image inside your book, on the cover, or for any online media, such as blog posts or social media images, make sure that you have permission to use the image. You can purchase stock photos, utilize websites that offer free stock photos, commission a photographer or artist, or take your own pictures.

Google it: Before you settle on a book title, search for that name or phrase online. Does it bring up another book? Is it related to something you don't want to be related to? Take a moment to Google your own name to see if there is another author with your name. If your first and last names are common, consider adding your middle or maiden name or initial. Some writers use a pen name. Before you settle on one, do a little internet research.

Formatting and Design: If you choose to indie publish your book, you will need to take charge of the formatting as well as the interior and cover design. You can hire someone else for these tasks or tackle them on your own. Helpful resources include the forums on Createspace.com and Facebook groups for independent authors. Seek input from others along the way. The books cover and page layout should look professional when you are done. If you work with a publishing company, they will probably direct these areas. However, it doesn't hurt to know what you want the book's cover to look like, so that you are prepared to give input.

You will likely come up with other questions as you write, edit, format, and publish. Research online, with books, in a writers' group or by contacting other authors.

Chapter 8: Who is Your Audience?

Usually you cannot simply write a book, make it available for purchase, and expect people to buy it. A used book website called ThriftBooks boasts that they have seven million titles listed. If there are millions of books available at the click of a mouse, how will someone find your book and why would they buy it? I don't ask these questions to intimidate you, but to prompt you to know your audience.

While you are writing your book, you should simultaneously build up your audience. When your book becomes available for sale, you need people to buy it! If nobody knows about your book and their appetites have not been whetted, it will be harder to get books into people's hands. There are authors who write very good books but nobody knows about them. I want to write because I'm called, but I also write because I have a message that I want people to read. Therefore, I need readers, and I must be making my writing known.

Who is your audience? This is an important question! If you're writing a children's book, what age are you targeting? Is it intended for a specific gender? Is it a Christian book or not? Who do you expect to read it?

If you're writing a full-length novel, who is your audience? Women? Men and women? Teenagers and adults, or just one or the other?

My first book flowed naturally out of our experience struggling to start our family. It was difficult to open up about a personal topic, but in hindsight, I am grateful that my debut publication was intended for a specific audience: it's targeted to people who are facing infertility. Several years after the book released I thank God that sales remain steady. Practical steps led to that book selling well. I focused on strategic marketing along with connecting with my target audience. You could say that I have "built a platform" through social media.

Platform?

For years, we have been told that we must have a platform before we can become published authors. Large publishers take into consideration the size of your social media following before they sign a contract. Indie publishers must have a way to promote their books, therefore they expect you to have a platform to self-promote.

As I was writing this book, author and speaker Beth Moore wrote a blog post[1] challenging the notion that Christian authors or speakers should be building a platform for themselves. She questions the concept of personal branding and self-promoting. She's right: it's not all about me, it's not all about you, it's not even about our message, no matter how biblical or Christ-centered that message is. As a Christian author, it's ultimately about Jesus. Are you glorifying yourself or glorifying God? Are you loving the idea of earning money from books, or are you loving Jesus? Are you stepping on and crushing fellow brothers and sisters in the faith as you climb to the top? Or are you doing all things in humility, that Christ may be glorified?

Remember that God, the Author and Creator, is the one who inspires our creative ideas. Our ideas come from Him. As Christians writing for God's glory, all things are from Him, and for Him. The ideas that I turn into books? Those came from God. The strength to finish a project and tell people about it? It comes from God. The messages I share based on His truth? Each one comes from Him. He's the one who inspires me, and He's the one I aim to glorify.

That being said, do I need a platform?

That's a question I'm wrestling with and you should consider it as well. If you want people to read your books, you need a way to reach them. You need an audience. But if you want to be great, if you want to be famous, if your goal is to win and you're a Christian, I encourage you to pause and re-evaluate.

It's not all about my success. It's not about you becoming great. Writing as a Christian shouldn't be about fame, money, or our own greatness. It should be about pointing people toward God, about sharing Christian values, and putting life-giving words before other people.

I expect that I will continue writing books until I die. It's part of who I am. I'm satisfied to slowly build my writing career. I don't need to have an extravagant platform. I don't need center stage. I'll be fine without hitting the *New York Times* best sellers list. I would be delighted if that happened, but I am okay simply writing and producing because that's what God has called me to do.

Where is your audience?

Where will you find readers for your book? Do you speak in front of groups? Speaking engagements provide opportunities to share your writing. Maybe you're a pastor or in a leadership role in your church and have an opportunity to share about your book in that venue.

Are you influential on social media? I think there is a fine line between aggravating your social media contacts and influencing them well. I'm certain that I have annoyed people and I've even been blocked and unfollowed. I post a mixture of cute pictures of the children I nanny, updates about what I'm doing, blog posts I've written, and words of encouragement for those in barren seasons. As you use social media, make sure you're talking about your day-to-day life and not just about your writing. Friends may feel turned off if your page is full of promotional material.

Sometimes I don't feel like I'm having any influence through social media, then I attended a reunion where several people came up to me to say how much they appreciated the encouraging words I had shared online. This helped me to realize that I am influencing people on social media.

I try to not be too annoying. I hold back on sharing many controversial things. I don't air my dirty laundry on the web. I am not always an upbeat and positive person, but that doesn't mean I need to be the Debbie Downer of social media. We can all use social media responsibly.

Writer vs. Speaker

As I worked on my first book, I realized that speaking and writing frequently go hand in hand – often a person is both a speaker and a writer. Public speakers write books, and authors speak to groups. I also noticed that most people are stronger in one area than the other. Some of my favorite speakers are people I could listen to for hours on end, but I have not enjoyed their blog posts or books. I suspect that the most gifted writers are not the best public speakers.

For the first couple of years after becoming an author, I wrestled with my sense of obligation to speak to groups. I assumed that this was how I should promote my books. If I speak to a group, people will help me spread the word and buy my books, right?

I felt the pressure to seek out speaking engagements. Not only did I not know where to begin, but I felt overwhelmed at the thought. I work more than forty hours a week at my day job, I write in my spare time, I need time to spend with my husband, plus many other obligations consume my time. How am I supposed to fit public speaking into my busy schedule?

One day I heard a Christian author share that she felt called to write more than to speak, so she was stepping down from speaking engagements to focus on family and writing. She realized that she was primarily a writer, not a speaker.

I heard these words while driving home from work, and the pressure immediately lifted. I'm a writer, not a speaker, I thought. At that moment, I decided to not pursue speaking engagements, but instead to simply welcome opportunities that were handed to me.

While attending an event just a few weeks later, someone said, "Would you like a few minutes with the microphone to talk about your new book?"

"Um, yes!" I replied.

Months later, I was asked to share my life story and my writing journey with a group of women. It was such a smooth time because it was a God-ordained time. There was no striving to pursue those two speaking opportunities, instead I simply walked through the doors opened for me.

I'm open to one day speaking to groups more frequently, if it's a joy and not a burden. If God opens the doors and adjusts my schedule to allow such opportunities, then I would be happy to speak more. However, my primary means of communication will likely be writing instead of public speaking.

Don't feel pressured one way or the other. Maybe your passion is speaking, and writing comes second. You need to walk that out as God directs you. If you feel that writing is your primary form of communication, then keep on writing your stories and let go of the pressure to speak to groups.

Each of us is unique in the way that we connect with other people. As writers who want other people to read our words, we must know who our current audience is, then find the best method of reaching them.

Chapter 9: Getting Real About Finances

I'm going to talk rather candidly in this section, to help launch you into your writing career with wisdom, hope, and realistic expectations.

Maybe you dream of having a career as an author. You want to earn a living writing books. You would love to be known as a best-selling author, to see your books on display in libraries and bookstores. Maybe you simply want your books to be your primary source of income. There are authors who earn their living by writing, right?

I dream right alongside you. A few years ago, my mom handed me a packet of miscellaneous papers from childhood and high school, including a standardized test I had taken as a teenager. I saw that I had selected "writer" as my career path. I took the long route to becoming a writer, working in ministry, emergency services, health insurance, and childcare before writing a book. I still work full-time, and I dream of one day having a primary role of wife-and-mom, with the secondary role of author. I dream of earning a significant income from my books.

But the fact is, earning an ample income from writing doesn't happen for all authors, and the majority of those who are earning from writing would tell you about the lean years as they began. In Stephen King's book *On Writing: A Memoir of the Craft* he shares that he didn't make much money from his writing for a long time. If you're one of the few who makes it big as a new author, congratulations! But if you find that writing does not earn a quick income, I think that you're in the majority.

Looking realistically at numbers, in the United States if you work 40 hours a week earning current minimum wage of $7.25, you'd earn $290 per week before tax.

Instead, let's say that as an author you earn $5 per book sold (which might be a generous number). You'd have to sell fifty-eight books per week to earn minimum wage. That means that you'll need to have a lot of venues selling your books, and it also means that you need to publish multiple books. The bottom line here is that very few authors of one book will be able to fully support themselves or their families from book sales.

Becoming an author is like having a second full-time job that pays in pennies. Recently I was feeling very discouraged about the long hours I was pouring into writing and the small amount of income it generated. While attending The Breath and the Clay[1] creative arts conference in North Carolina, I had a complete change in my perspective on this matter.

A panel of artists, including writers, musicians, and visual artists, were answering questions that the audience had submitted. One of the questions had to do with money. John Mark McMillan, a Christian musician, responded with a question of his own.

"Are you willing to support your art, even if your art doesn't support you?" he asked the audience. He then commented that not everyone will earn a living from their art. Another artist chimed in that she had been told to give her art five years before evaluating her success.

I took a deep breath, and everything changed. No longer did I feel bogged down with the classic financial struggle of a starving artist. I decided that I can strategically manage the finances of my books so that writing them is a joy and not a drain. Yes, I'm willing to support my work as a writer with my day job. I'm willing to write, even if it doesn't pay well.

I came home from the conference and tallied up my income from books, discovering that although I worked on writing nearly every day, and some days for many hours, for the past couple of years I was only earning a couple of dollars per day.

Is it because I've chosen to be an indie author? Or is it because writing doesn't pay much in the beginning? I don't know the answer, but I do know that I feel called to write, even if my effort doesn't immediately pay me back.

Realistic Expectations

I live just outside of Washington, D.C., in a very high cost of living area. Jobs in and near D.C. typically pay better than those in other parts of the country because housing costs are very high. Whether I'm a writer living in the rolling hills of Tennessee or in a tiny flat in D.C., my books will sell for a similar price across the country. It's hard to earn an income solely as an author in D.C. In my minimum wage example above, I suspect that it's tough to earn a living as a new author in most places.

Years ago, I was working in the Customer Service department for a health insurance company. When I was a child, dreaming of becoming an author, I'm certain that answering phones for an insurance company was never my dream. Does anyone dream of working for an insurance company?

While working at the insurance company, I read *The Other 8 Hours: Maximize Your Free Time to Create New Wealth & Purpose* by Robert Pagliarini[2]. It was one of the most transformative books I have ever encountered, and I highly recommend that you read it as well. The gist of the book is this: most people work eight hours and sleep eight hours, which leaves eight more hours in each day. How are you using your other eight hours to pursue your dreams?

While working in health insurance, I knew that I wanted to transition into a childcare job, with hopes that I could be a stay-at-home-mom and care for other people's children to earn some extra income. I babysat regularly while working for the insurance company. The day came when my husband and I decided to move from North Carolina to the Washington, D.C. suburbs, and those families gave a positive reference to the family I began nannying. Those hours of babysitting I logged while working at the insurance company built my resume so that I could be a confident and competent full-time nanny.

Then, while working long hours as a nanny, I began pursuing my dream of being an author. The principle of using those "other eight hours" wisely has allowed me to pursue new dreams while earning an income in a stable job.

Right now, I feel like I have two full-time jobs: childcare and writing. Working as a nanny gives me the benefit of a work schedule, people for my extroverted self to interact with, hands-on work that does not involve a computer or writing, and a steady paycheck. I also enjoy the fun times and hugs from little children. Writing provides an intellectual outlet, a ministry, and an opportunity to pursue my lifelong dream of being an author. Yes, I essentially work two jobs, but I don't have the pressure of needing to earn a certain amount from writing. Therefore, my writing career is a joy, and it's one I can support, even if it's not supporting me. I hope for a day when the tables turn and I earn a significant amount from writing, yet I'm glad that I am not forced to write because I need the money.

In my writers' group, those who write as part of their day job struggle to find the creativity and energy to write at home. If writing is the art you're going to support, consider other ways to earn an income to support your writing. For me, it's childcare. Have you considered a manual job such as cleaning or lawncare? That type of work might not seem glamorous, but there can be advantages for writers or creative artists. Manual jobs might pay sufficiently on an hourly basis. If you're cleaning buildings or mowing yards or driving as a courier, then you are not sitting at a computer, so when you do sit down to write, you're not already feeling burned out. You can ponder your ideas while you're working. You can move around during your job, instead of being stuck in a cubicle. Then your body is ready to sit at a desk and write your dreams. Maybe these job options aren't right for you, but maybe they'll work for someone. Regardless of what you choose, I suggest that you find an income-providing job that doesn't drain your creative energy while you write books.

Stick to a Budget

As I talk about "supporting my art," I want to stress the importance of not overspending before you start earning money from your books. It's wise to stay within your budget, keeping costs as low as possible. Some new authors pay too much for a publishing deal or for advertisement, they purchase too many books in bulk, and spend way too much money in the process of preparing a book for release, assuming they'll earn it back quickly.

Set a budget for your first book launch and stay within your budget. Consider using only the earnings from your first book to fund your second book's launch. Regardless of how you go about it, make wise decisions with your publishing and launching finances and don't make the mistake of overspending on the front end. Eventually as you continue to write and sell books, your income hopefully will grow.

While writing and publishing my first book, I hoped that selling the books would help to supplement our income. During the writing and publishing process, we were working with a budget close to zero. My costs were minimal as a new indie author, and friends and family contributed to the project with photography, cover design, editing, and marketing. Without a team of people helping us out, that book would not have made it into many hands. I'm forever grateful for the team that helped me birth my first book.

Re-focus

I don't recommend launching a writing career to make money. I do suggest writing books because you love books and because you have a desire or calling to write one. I might have a dream of being an author who earns a living by writing, but I have a greater dream of positively impacting lives with my writing. Therefore, I continue to write and I continue to produce books because that is what God has directed me to do. I find joy in the writing process, and I hope that my words encourage and impact others.

I'll be honest, I do feel discouraged after a month with very few sales. I sometimes wonder if it's worth all the effort. Sometimes I'm simply wondering, "How do I promote this book?" While writing this, I was feeling that way about my first children's book, realizing that I simply don't know the best strategies for getting a children's book into people's hands.

Then I received a video message from a college classmate, saying that her young child was loving my book. I watched this little one read the book out loud, just as I would read it, and I realized that the message of the book is sinking into this child's heart. My hope is that when these kids grow up and face more difficult seasons, a phrase will echo in their minds, "Yes, my God is good, all of the time, in all seasons of life He'll never change." I wrote that book so that children will ponder God's goodness for the rest of their lives. I did not write that book to earn a lot of money.

Similar moments of encouragement have happened with my book *Embracing Hope During Infertility*. I wonder if anyone is reading it, and then I receive a message from a stranger telling me that it has helped her. Did I write that book for my own fame, or to help hurting women?

In moments like that, I see my books doing what they're designed to do. That is why I write. As you prepare to publish your books, make sure you count the cost so that writing is a joy.

Chapter 10: How Do I Get Published?

Many people dreaming of writing a book find themselves stuck on the question: "How will I get published?"

It's much easier to publish a book today than it was twenty years ago, thanks to the indie publishing industry and print-on-demand capabilities. Please note that I live in the United States, so much of this chapter will apply to books published here. I hear that Canada has similar, yet different options, and publishing options will vary in other parts of the world.

Have you noticed how in the past century, many industries have gone from small business to large corporation, and then small again? Small farm, then large food company, now we're back to support-your-local-farmer. One-room schoolhouse, large public school, now many are homeschooling and using a community co-op. Traditional taxis are now competing with individual Uber drivers.

In many areas of modern civilization, small is the new large. I see publishing like that. Currently, I have chosen to self-publish as an indie author, and I am very comfortable with that choice. Not everyone wants to take the plunge and independently publish, so there are several options to consider.

How will you publish your book? Options include the following publishers: Large traditional publishing houses, small publishing houses, small indie publishers, and completely independently.

Large Publishing House

When you walk into a chain bookstore such as Barnes & Noble, most books that you see are published by large, traditional publishing companies. Some big names include Penguin Random House or HarperCollins. Well-known Christian publishers include Zondervan, Thomas Nelson, or Baker House.

Publishing through a traditional company has been the primary way books have been published for decades. Most people would prefer to be published by a big-name publisher. However, there are several things to keep in mind as you consider this option.

First, for your book to be considered by most publishers, you must have an agent. If an agent takes you on as a client, they will pitch your book to publishing houses. It's rare that a big-name publisher will accept a manuscript submitted directly by the author. Only a very small number of manuscripts considered by large publishing houses are published.

These companies also expect first-time authors to already have a large platform, or audience, because they want to be ensured that readers will buy the book.

Large publishers offer several benefits. They pay you, they help you get the word out there, and they offer your books in bookstores and online.

Negatives of working with a large publisher include the pace of the process. As I finished writing my first book, I wanted to publish it as soon as possible. I did not want to wait for month after month for an agent to review it, then for a publisher to consider it. Once a publisher accepts a book, it can take one to two more years before that book is released. If you don't feel a sense of urgency, and you want to be published by a big publisher, then keep working toward getting an agent and getting your foot in the door with a publisher.

If you attend a writing conference, seek opportunities to meet with an agent there. If you know someone who has an agent, ask how to get connected. Do your research online. Read books such as *Jeff Herman's Guide to Book Publishers, Editors and Literary Agents 2017: Who They Are, What They Want, How to Win Them Over* by Jeff Herman[1].

Keep in mind that large publishers will have a lot of say about the publishing process, including what you write and when your book is published. For example, I saw a Facebook post by a well-known author who was finishing a manuscript. In that post she shared the title she had given her upcoming book, then weeks later the publisher announced her book with an entirely different name. A friend of mine submitted her manuscript to a large publishing house, and the publisher recommended that she change her setting of the story from one part of the world to another, which would entirely change her storyline. The author gains much from working with a large publisher, but they lose a lot of power and potential royalties.

When using a large publisher, there are more middlemen to be paid. The bookstore gains a profit, the publishing company earns from your book, as does the agent. When you publish independently, you lose some advantages offered by big publishers, but you are not paying the middleman.

While writing my first book, I began researching these publishing options. I felt strongly that my book needed to be published quickly, without waiting for a large publisher. Also, while writing a very emotional memoir, I didn't feel like I had the stamina to pursue agents, knowing there was a good chance I would be rejected. I considered paying a small independent publisher, which is an option many people are happy with.

Small Publishing House

A smaller traditional publishing house offers some of the perks of a large publisher, but might require some of the fees you would pay a small independent publisher (also known as a vanity press). Small publishing companies have a greater ability of getting your books into a bookstore. They will help promote your book, and your book will bear the imprint of a publishing company. (Small publishing houses often promote their books in traditional bookstores as well as online. There can be a fine line between a small publishing house and a company you would pay to self-publish your book. When considering publishers, find out if they are established in bookstores and ask what out of pocket cost is required of you.)

If you choose a small publisher, I would recommend that you first look at the other books they've published. Contact an author who has used their services to see what he or she recommends.

If you hope to become published with a large publisher one day, publishing through a smaller press demonstrates that you're up for the challenge of working with an editor and publisher.

There are cons to a small publisher as well. Even though they offer some of the benefits of a large publisher, they will likely charge you fees up front to publish your book. Each author must research the cost and decide if it is worth the benefits.

Also, I've known more than one author who has published with a small publisher, then watched in dismay as that company abruptly went out of business. Publishing is a competitive marketplace, so if you choose to self-publish with a small publisher, please be aware that this could happen.

Small publishing houses as well as small indie publishers may require you to purchase copies of your book in bulk, leading some authors to have a basement full of books that they must sell.

Small Indie Publisher

These publishers are a hybrid between a small traditional publisher and an independent publishing company. Sometimes this type of publishing is called a vanity press. Essentially you will hire this company to self-publish your book. The advantages to this method are that the publisher will help design your cover, format your book, provide editing services, and help you promote it. However, you will pay a fee for these services. Do your research to determine if this is the right route for you.

The following companies advertise as self-publishing companies:

WestBow Press[2] http://www.westbowpress.com/

IngramSpark[3] http://www.ingramspark.com/ (Some indie authors use a combination of IngramSpark and CreateSpace.)

Lulu[4] https://www.lulu.com/

BookBaby[5] www.bookbaby.com

Xulon[6] http://www.xulonpress.com/

I'm sure there are more self-publishing companies available, but these have come to my attention in recent years. Before you commit, do some research, and ask questions of others who have used that company. If you don't know anyone personally, find the forums on the web, or join an indie author discussion group on Facebook.

Independent Publishing (also called Indie or Self-Publishing)

In my early twenties, Starbucks was the newest place to hangout in our town. Next to the cash register I saw CDs for sale, often advertised as "indie music." I had no idea what "indie music" was, but I thought it looked cool.

Well, here I am, now an "indie author." I finally learned that indie simply refers to music or writing produced without a record label or a publisher. I am my own publisher, I don't use an agent or publishing house, so I am an indie published author. I will use the terms self-publishing and indie-publishing interchangeably.

At this point, I'm confident that indie is the right choice for me, and although it's not the route everyone will take, I enjoy sharing why I chose this path and how I'm doing it. (That's why I'm writing this book: I want to remind aspiring authors that nothing needs to stop them from writing and publishing the book that's on their hearts.)

When you self-publish, there are several ways to go about it. One option is to create an e-book as a PDF, allowing readers to download it from your website. This electronic download, created on your computer, is one you can choose to sell or give away. I have never done this, so I cannot speak from personal experience. I do not enjoy reading books in PDF form, so I've never bought one of these.

Another way to publish is to independently publish through Amazon's platforms: CreateSpace[7] for paperback and KDP (Kindle Direct Publishing)[8] for Kindle. Like it or not, it seems that Amazon currently dominates the e-book market. Up-front costs are very low, and this publishing avenue offers authors an opportunity to reach the world. This is how I have chosen to publish my books, and I love it. Some indie authors also publish their books through Barnes & Noble's Nook, iBooks, Kobo, and Google Play.

A perk to publishing through CreateSpace is the print-on-demand technology. I am not required to buy books in bulk, although I occasionally purchase copies to have on hand. Amazon also does not need to store my books in a warehouse. When a customer orders a book published through CreateSpace, Amazon prints the book and mails it to the customer. (This entire process of printing and shipping can happen within the 2-day window of Amazon Prime delivery.)

Using CreateSpace and/or KDP can be very inexpensive or even free, and the process is relatively simple. Once you have finished writing and editing your book, you will need to format it, or hire someone to format it properly. I choose to format my own books, however many authors I have met pay someone else to do the formatting. E-books and paper copies have different formatting requirements. Do your research, and if you're not comfortable trying to format your own, then hire someone.

If you publish a paper copy, you'll need to choose the size of the book. Do you want your pages to be bright white or off-white? Do you want your book's cover to be matte or glossy? (Once again, throughout your writing process build relationships with other authors both in person and through social media. They will be able to point you in the right direction with your questions.)

In the United States, you can publish using CreateSpace as your imprint. You also have the option of purchasing your own ISBN numbers through Bowker, and by doing so you can name your own imprint. I prefer to not have the CreateSpace label on my books, so I have purchased my own ISBNs.

Another aspect to consider is the cover of your book. If you're working with a small or large publisher, they will play a part in cover design. If you're an indie author, you can choose whether to design your own cover or to hire a designer. Anyone with basic graphic design skills can follow the guidelines you'll find on the CreateSpace or KDP website, however, people do judge books by their covers, so you want to be sure it looks professional. Ask others for honest feedback before finalizing your cover design.

Once your book has been formatted and your cover is ready, you upload both through your CreateSpace or KDP account. Someone on the other end reviews it, and often within a matter of days, your book is ready to go. I recommend ordering a proof copy of your paperback to be sure it looks as good as you imagine it will. Once you've seen it, you click the final button, and typically within a few days your book will be available online.

Publishing through CreateSpace allows you to make your book available on Amazon (in several countries), as well as through "expanded distribution" which currently includes websites such as BarnesandNoble.com, BooksAMillion.com, and Walmart.Com. The simplicity of this process is that you receive a monthly payment from CreateSpace and KDP.

Some authors sell books through their website. Some sell them in person at events. If you choose to sell your books this way, research the tax laws to make sure you are handling the transactions by law.

The primary downside to CreateSpace is that it's tough to get books published through them into bookstores. However, these books are available on Amazon and can be ordered online or in-store at box stores like Barnes & Noble.

Getting into bookstores

Bookstores want to be sure that they can sell your books. They want to be convinced that customers will walk in their doors to buy your books before they stock them on the shelves. If the books don't sell, large chain bookstores want to know that they can return the excess books to the publisher. Unfortunately, bookstores prefer to work with large, trusted publishers, for this reason. Therefore, it's difficult for indie authors or small publisher authors to get their books into bookstores.

However, you can work with a manager directly to discuss the possibility of selling your books, or to ask if you could hold a book signing in their store.

What will your book look like?

Especially if you decide to self-publish, these are options you need to consider. Will your book be paperback or hardback? What size? Do you want your paper to be bright white or off-white? Will it be an e-book for Kindle or another brand, or simply a PDF e-book that people can download straight from your website?

What will your book cost? I am a reader, and I enjoy reading a lot of books without spending a significant amount of money on them. I don't have a lot of bookshelf space left at home, and I haven't gotten rich from writing yet. Therefore, I prefer to read library books or Kindle books that cost less than four dollars. With access to used books, a huge public library, and an eye for Kindle deals, I don't spend a lot of money on books, although it's my goal to read 50 books each year. When I see an average-length paperback book selling for above $15, it's highly unlikely that I will buy it. I was required to buy too many overpriced books as a college student, and I hope that my expensive textbook days are over!

I understand that authors want to make money on their books, but my hunch is that we will sell more books at $12 each than we would at $18. It is more important to me to put books into the hands of readers than to earn an extra couple of dollars per book. If you're working with a publishing house, it's likely that they will determine the price. If you're independently publishing, take into consideration the prices suggested by CreateSpace or KDP. Don't make yourself look cheap, but don't overprice your books either. If you are using independent platforms, you can experiment with your price over the course of time to see what price point sells best.

A tremendous advantage to indie publishing is that you control your price. I'm an avid reader. Borrowing books from the library is my first choice, buying Kindle books is my second, and purchasing paperbacks is reserved for special occasions. Indie authors have a low overhead since they're not paying the middlemen such as an agent or publishing company, and therefore the prices are often more reasonable. Many times, I see books published through small publishers that are priced higher than I want to pay – especially Kindle books. Indie authors have more control of their prices, they can choose when to put a book on sale, and determine the cost at any given time.

If you choose to self-publish, you can offer your Kindle book for free, either for a period of time or all of the time. Some authors find that offering the first novel in a series for free helps to sell the rest of the series. When I launched my first book, the e-book was free for a few days to get it into as many hands as possible. If enough readers purchase or download a copy, Amazon might recommend your book as a "hot new release" and it's fun to see your book featured in that category!

Chapter 11: Marketing and Launching

Before I began writing my first book, I stopped by my local post office one Saturday to mail a package at the self-service kiosk. The man waiting to use the postage machine after me told me that he was an author, and that he was there to mail a couple of books people had ordered. He pulled out a copy to show me and named the price, offering to sell me a book on the spot. Although the historical account looked interesting, I declined. Years later, as an author, I understand a couple of things better. First, people write books because they're passionate about a topic, and they want you to read their books. Second, authors must work hard to sell their books regardless of whether they published independently or through a big publisher.

The process of writing a book is like being pregnant with an idea. Finishing the project and publishing it is like the birthing process. Although it can be painful or difficult, giving birth to your book is worth it. As a writer, we might think that once we publish we're done, right?

As any mother knows, giving birth is just the beginning. Just as it's up to you to nurture and teach your child, you still must "raise" your book. There is much post-publication nurturing to be done for a book. You must market or promote your book to get it into people's hands.

At the very first writer's conference I attended, I learned that whether an author uses a publishing company or independently publishes, the author will still be responsible to promote his or her own work. Even with a large publishing company backing you up, you as the author will be the primary person marketing the book.

I have yet to meet an author who loves self-promoting. I'm an extrovert, but introverted enough to want to spend hours alone writing. (Maybe it's my extroverted self that has taken me to the local library and a nearby café to continue this writing session, instead of being home alone.) Nevertheless, many writers are introverts who don't enjoy marketing.

Many of us are writing books because writing is how communicate best, and because we want to write, not focus on selling. I often say, if I wanted a career in sales and marketing, I would be in sales and marketing, not nannying and writing. However, the reality is that all authors must promote their books.

Have you ever heard a conference speaker begin their talk by telling you what's on their resource table in the lobby? Maybe they throw a t-shirt or a book out to the crowd, because they want you to go buy their resources. Every author wants people to buy their books, but many (if not most) authors, don't feel comfortable saying, "HEY! GO BUY MY BOOKS!"

Many years ago, I heard about an author who apparently wrote very good novels, but she was very timid and didn't want to self-promote, and therefore very few people read her books. On the flip side, I've encountered social media friends who are very pushy about a product they sell, and I cringe when their posts and messages come across my screen because they're trying so hard to sell me a product I do not want. We must find the balance between being silent and overbearing. As an author who would like to earn money from her books, I am constantly learning the art of getting the word out there without overwhelming my audience or driving them away.

Promoting vs. Advertising

One difference between promoting and advertising is remembering that people typically pay for advertisements, while promotions can be free or very inexpensive. Paid advertising is certainly an option, although it's wise to consider your budget.

You can pay to advertise on social media sites, Amazon, and Google, to name a few. If you're counting the cost, and don't want to throw all your money into advertisement, consider focusing on promotions instead. Here are some options for free or inexpensive promotions of your book.

Promoting

In this section, you'll find many suggestions for book promotion. This is not an exhaustive list, and you do not need to do everything I suggest. However, if you want your book to reach your audience, you need to promote it.

To promote your book in this generation, it's important to have an online presence. Do you have a blog or website? If you don't know where to start, ask friends and family for suggestions. Find an online course, such as one offered by Amy Lynn Andrews[1] https://amylynnandrews.com/. You can set up a free site through Blogger or Wordpress. I would recommend purchasing your own domain name through a company like GoDaddy or Hover.

Authors should also have a mailing list. MailChimp is one of several good avenues you can use to create a free email newsletter. I have personally been slow to embrace this, but every author I've heard from recommends it.

It's good to have a professional quality headshot to use online. When your book becomes available on Amazon.com, set up an Amazon Author Page[2] here: https://authorcentral.amazon.com/.

Many avid readers track what they're reading on Goodreads[3], so set up an author profile there as well, and make sure that your book is listed: https://www.goodreads.com/author/program.

Learn how to use social media sites well. Personal preference, age, and trends seem to determine where various people post, but consider using Facebook, Instagram, Twitter, and Pinterest as avenues for gaining visibility. If you're comfortable making videos, get a YouTube channel and share your videos on social media. Some writers use Google+ or LinkedIn. You should consider setting up a professional social media page along with your personal account.

If you have the resources or know someone willing to help, create a book trailer for your book. This is a short video, like a movie trailer, that you can share online. It would describe your book and briefly interview you as the author.

Ask for endorsements. I felt too insecure to consider this with my first book, but I intend to include endorsements in this book. Ask fellow authors, readers, speakers, leaders, teachers, or anyone connected to the genre of your book to pre-read it and write a short endorsement. If you plan to ask an established author who you do not know personally, you'll need to sell them on the idea of reading and endorsing your book. With your request, let them know that they would be doing you a huge favor, and express your appreciation to them. Some people will not have the time to endorse your writing, but receive what you can.

Inquire at your local library. Will they accept a donation of your book? Will they allow you to do a reading or a book signing? Don't be afraid to ask.

Does your church have a newsletter or social media site or any place where you can announce the release of your book? You could send an update to your university's alumni newsletter, announcing that you have published a book.

Ask blogger friends if they would be willing to do a giveaway of your book. This is a good way to spread the word on social media and bring the book to people's attention.

Set up a table at a local fair or festival. Fall is a good time for craft shows and vendor fairs, but sign-ups can begin late in the spring. Inquire about setting up at a church or school event. In my area, Methodist churches seem to host these more than any other churches. Most of these events require a fee to set up a booth, so make sure you can expect to earn back the fee with your sales. Some authors set up at book conventions. Once again, take the cost into account, and keep in mind that your book will be competing with hundreds or thousands of others.

Seek opportunities to do book readings or presentations, if that's something you have the time and ability to pursue. Like I said earlier, at the time I released my first book I felt obligated to seek speaking engagements but lacked the time and emotional energy. Realizing that this was not my priority was freeing.

When I published my first children's book, I went to several preschool classrooms to read the book aloud. A children's author I met recently recommended that one of the best ways to promote a children's book is to read to classrooms. There is no cost, and the school will notify the parents, who might buy the book.

Request Amazon reviews and other online reviews. When readers say that they finished read your book, thank them, and ask them to leave a review on Amazon. All reviews are vital. Authors need reviews, both good and bad, to provide feedback and illustrate the quality of our work.

Watching *Shark Tank* on TV helps to generate marketing ideas in my brain. This show involves entrepreneurs presenting their ideas to investors. Authors, in a sense, are entrepreneurs, presenting our ideas in book form, hoping that people will buy them. Watching *Shark Tank* helps me to gauge good and bad marketing, and it helps me to think about the finances and investment that go into book writing. I want to earn money, not lose money, as an author, and watching this show helps me think from the perspective of a businesswoman.

More ways to promote your book include sending out a press release, doing an interview on a podcast, and networking with writers' groups and book clubs.

Through the internet, you can find many websites and people willing to coach you in writing, publishing, and launching. Learn from them, but continue to watch your budget. You don't need to buy every class or resource out made available by those who claim to guarantee abundant book sales.

Advertising

You can pay to advertise your book on social media. Facebook regularly offers to sell me ads, and I regularly decline.

If you publish through a small publisher or paid indie publisher, they may offer you opportunities to consider, such as paying for social media ads or book trailers. Going back to my thoughts on wisely budgeting, please thoroughly research each option to make sure it will benefit you. If possible, ask someone who has used these resources to see if the return on investment is worth it.

Business cards are a practical way to promote yourself. Websites like Vistaprint will print them inexpensively. You can order business cards from higher-end websites as well. When I finally ordered cards that said Author below my name, the title felt more real.

Bookmarks or small cards advertising your book are fun, and they look nice on a display. Once again, I suggest considering your budget. How many books will you need to sell to pay for your bookmarks?

Other promo items like pens or magnets are fun to offer, but only if they fit into your budget.

Launching

Marketing your book successfully begins with launching it well. Your launch day, or release day, is the day your book is first available for sale. You should build anticipation in your readers for weeks or months in advance, and you want to come out of the gate with a bang. This is good for the publicity of your book, and it's good for the author's morale too.

After all the time and energy authors pour into the writing, editing, and publishing of a book, the day comes to launch it out into the world. Like me, you might find yourself exhausted, saying something like, "I just want to give birth to this thing and be done!" However, a strong launch is important. You want your book to make a splash, to get into people's hands, and to be well-received by readers.

If you are working with a publisher, they will likely have a say in how you launch your book. They might offer suggestions, a timeline, or assistance. It's likely that they will choose the release day of your book.

If you are independently publishing a book, take note of this section because you need to strategically plan your launch.

Regardless of how your book is published, the bulk of promoting and marketing the book is in the hands of the author. This book is your baby and you want it to go far and do great things.

Choose a launch day

Often books, music, and DVDs are released on Tuesdays. Will that same day of the week work for your schedule?

Can you, or should you, time your release around holidays? Most of the time it's probably not a good idea, as readers are focused on the holiday, instead of sitting down to read. However, there may be certain items that sell well around specific holidays. We launched *Seasons: A Picture Book* just before Thanksgiving, hoping that people would take advantage of holiday shopping, and they did. Research has shown that certain books sell better at designated times of the year.

For example, the Self-Publishing Advice Center[4] outlines genres in this list: https://selfpublishingadvice.org/timing-for-book-launches/. They list the following:

- January-April: Romance, Self-help, Business, Cookbooks
- May-August: Adventure, Fantasy, Travel
- September-November: Academic, Horror, Paranormal
- December-January: Children, Cookery, Illustrated, Quiz, Dictionaries, and Quirky Fun Books

As a reader, I would agree that people are more likely to read fiction while sitting on the beach in the summer, and they're more motivated to dig into a weight-loss guide in January while making New Year's resolutions.

You are not locked into releasing your book on a certain day of the week or time of the year, but you should take note that the book industry has a way of doing so. Use the internet to research your questions as you prepare to launch your book.

I also suggest remembering your launch day is tentative until you're just a week or two away from it. Each time I launch a book I have run into logistical hurdles that have slowed me down. Yet prior to each launch, I've told my social media followers about it a week or two in advance.

Create a launch team

You should work on this months before the launch, depending on how long it will take people to read your book and how soon you plan to release it. I've participated in several and facilitated one. A launch team can be in communication with you and each other through a private Facebook group that you set up. (If you have a knowledgeable friend willing to facilitate the launch team, let them do so.) In that group, you can encourage your team to read through your book prior to the launch. Typically, the author provides the launch team with a PDF copy of the book. The launch team is expected to then share about your book on social media and they're highly encouraged to write a review upon release. Your launch team is made up of volunteers, and you can find them through your social media circles, your blog following, or through your real-life friends. I suggest that you include people that you do not know personally, such as social media contacts.

Throw a launch party

When I published *Embracing Hope During Infertility* one cold January, I felt emotionally spent, like I had nothing left to give. Although I had dreamed of having a launch party, it simply didn't work out, primarily because I was emotionally spent after publishing such a personal book. Nearly two years later when *Seasons: A Picture Book* was released, I had a fun illustrator working by my side and a dear friend who opened up her home for the party. One Sunday afternoon we offered cookies and hot beverages, and invited everyone we knew to drop by to celebrate the release of our children's book. We sold and signed books, and we enjoyed chatting with our guests. We had a delightful time. This was a wonderful way to celebrate the birth of a book. (While planning for the party, I was describing the concept of a launch party to a child I know, who replied, "So it's kind of like a baby shower for your book?" Yes, that's a good way to put it!)

That launch party was a lot of fun. However, it took time to prepare for and plan, and it subtracted energy from our already busy lives during a hustling holiday season. It also costs money to provide food and supplies; if you rent a venue or pay a lot for a launch party, keep in mind that it can eat up your earnings from book sales. Once again, I recommend keeping your budget in mind and considering low-cost ways to host a launch party. Will a coffee shop or bookstore allow you to have your party there? Then guests can buy their own drinks and you are not obligated to pay for their food. Decorations and party favors such as bookmarks are fun, but make sure they're not taking away too much of your earnings.

Social Media and Networking

If there is one time to risk annoying your social media contacts with talk about your books, it's launch week. Don't be the person who only uses their Facebook account to talk about the product you sell. Don't let sales dominate your posts, but in the days surrounding your launch you want to post a lot. Those who are overwhelmed can unfollow you for a while, but a social media contact may need to see your book posts several times before they actually click on the link to order. (Think about it, people scroll through Facebook at all hours of the day and night. They see one of your book release posts as they're falling asleep on Monday night. Tuesday morning when they're taking a bathroom break at work they see another post but don't have time to order. It might be that post they see when they're relaxing after dinner that reminds them to click the link and order your book.)

Launch week is an important time to send an email or two to your email list of subscribers. Consider also sending a personal email to friends and family, letting them know that your book is available for sale.

As you share about your book, ask others to help you spread the word. Those who have hundreds or thousands of Facebook friends, or those who seem to network well through social media would be ideal people to share about your book.

Chapter 12: You are an Author!

If you read this book from start to finish, it's likely that you're a writer who has a message to present or a story to tell. However, I believe that you're not just a writer: you are an author, and you are a pioneer. You're a step ahead of the wagon train, blazing the trail. You're not just holding the map, you're writing it.

As a pioneer, you will face obstacles, whether you experience writer's block due to lack of sleep, or whether you're wrestling with discouragement about the whole process.

If God has placed a message on your heart and prompted you to write your story, then you should keep going. Pioneer the trail He has set before you. He is the light to your path. He's the One directing your steps. Even if you feel intimidated or unqualified, if you are called to persevere as a writer, then press forward.

Don't fear the thought of sharing your story from the middle. Even if your circumstances aren't yet looking like a fairytale happy ending, you can still tell your life's story. You never know when your experiences or insights might be the key to someone else's breakthrough. Your words might offer the healing that a reader needs. Your story is valuable, and if God is prompting you to write and share it, trust that He will make your path clear.

In this generation, you can do so much more than write words on paper. With computers, technology, voice-to-text, the internet, social media, self-publishing, e-books, and print-on-demand publishing, it has never been easier to publish a book.

You may become an award winner or best seller, or you might not. But if your book impacts one life or many, is it worth it?

Looking back at my personal account of infertility that I published for the world to read, I firmly say "yes" to that question. The blood, sweat, and tears are worth it when I know others have been able to face their own journey with more hope. The fear of the unknown is worth it. On the days when I feel like a weary pioneer, it's worth it.

While writing this book, I repeatedly listened to a song called "Pioneer," recorded by Rick Pino. It became my anthem as I designed this map, with hopes that you too will voice your story, that you will launch your life-giving words into a world that needs to read them.

My hope is that all who read this book will stand on my shoulders, that your books are bigger and better than mine, that I inspire you to write. I hope that you go far in your writing career. If this little book brings forth your book, then it's worth my efforts. It is my honor to help pioneer your path. I encourage you to take some time, to sit down, and *Write Your Story*.

Thank you for reading this book.

Would you do me a tremendous favor?

I would be grateful if you'd write a quick review on Amazon or another online retailer. I also would appreciate if you recommend this book to others, either in person or through social media. Thank you!

You may contact me directly at betsyhermanauthor@gmail.com and join our Facebook group for more questions and answers: https://www.facebook.com/groups/writeyourstorygroup/.

About the author:

Betsy Herman lives in the Washington, D.C. area, where she works as a childcare provider and author. She and her husband Mike have been married for nine years, and they're happy to be expecting their first child. Together they enjoy exploring new cities on foot, eating at their favorite restaurants, and doing life as a team. Even though she sometimes wishes that she lived in the *Little House on the Prairie* days, she is grateful to be pioneering here and now.

You'll find more of her writing here:

www.lovethatbetsy.com

www.hopeduringinfertility.com

Acknowledgments

Thank you to my husband, Mike, for supporting my calling as a writer by giving me writing time and valuable feedback.

To the Unlocking Words writers, I am grateful for each of you. I value your friendship and appreciate your support.

Special thanks to these authors and artists for your nuggets of wisdom that have helped me along the way: Cathy Harris, Suzanne K. Lee, Elizabeth Maddrey, Bethany Kaczmarek, and Stephen Roach.

I couldn't have written this book without feedback from friends and beta readers. Juli, Don, Cathy, Suzanne, Markus, Gina, Tom, Martha, and Jennifer, thank you for reading my rough drafts and helping my words come to life!

Gina Green, your words spoke life into this project. You were the first to read *Write Your Story* and I appreciate your encouragement throughout the process!

Tom Smedley, as you edited this manuscript you caught my errors, made me sound more intelligent, and the notes you jotted throughout let me know that there is indeed an audience which can benefit from my writing. I am so grateful.

To my sister and brother-in-law, thank you both for brainstorming title and cover design ideas.

Rebekah Hauck, thank you for sharing your cover design skills.

Notes and Resources

Chapter 4: Sit Down and Write

    1.   Scrivener www.literatureandlatte.com/scrivener

Chapter 5: How?

    1.   Brian Tracy, *Eat That Frog! 21 Great Ways to Stop Procrastinating and Get More Done in Less Time* (Oakland, California: Berrett-Koehler Publishers, Inc., 2017)

    2.   Mason Currey, *Daily Rituals: How Artists Work* (New York: Random House, 2013)

    3.   Goodreads www.goodreads.com

    4.   American Christian Fiction Writers https://www.acfw.com/

    5.   Stephen King, *On Writing: A Memoir of the Craft* (New York, New York: Pocket Books, 2000)

    6.   Anna Whiston-Donaldson, *Rare Bird: A Memoir of Loss and Love* (United States: Convergent Books, 2014)

Chapter 6: These Struggles are Real

    1.   Kobi Yamada, *What Do You Do With an Idea?* (China: Compendium, Inc., 2013)

Chapter 7: Editing

    1.   Editorial Freelancers Association website www.the-efa.org (Lists estimated prices for editors.)
    2.   Lauren Graham, *Talking as Fast as I Can: From Gilmore Girls to Gilmore Girls (and Everything in Between)* (New York: Ballantine Books, 2016)
    3.   Copyright.gov https://www.copyright.gov/

Chapter 8: Who is Your Audience?

    1.   Beth Moore's blog post: https://blog.lproof.org/2017/04/personal-branding-conversation.html

Chapter 9: Getting Real About Finances

    1.   The Breath and the Clay http://www.thebreathandtheclay.com/
    2.   Robert Pagliarini, *The Other 8 Hours: Maximize Your Free Time to Create New Wealth & Purpose* (New York: St. Martin's Press, 2010)

Chapter 10: How Do I Get Published?

    1.   Jeff Herman, *Jeff Herman's Guide to Book Publishers, Editors and Literary Agents 2017: Who They Are, What They Want, How to Win Them Over* (Canada: New World Library, 2016)
    2.   WestBow Press http://www.westbowpress.com/
    3.   IngramSpark http://www.ingramspark.com/
    4.   Lulu https://www.lulu.com/
    5.   BookBaby www.bookbaby.com
    6.   Xulon http://www.xulonpress.com/
    7.   CreateSpace https://www.createspace.com/

8. Kindle Direct Publishing
https://kdp.amazon.com/en_US/

Chapter 11: Marketing and Launching

1. Amy Lynn Andrews
https://amylynnandrews.com/
2. Amazon Author Page
https://authorcentral.amazon.com/
3. Goodreads
https://www.goodreads.com/author/program
4. Self-Publishing Advice Center outlines genres in this list: https://selfpublishingadvice.org/timing-for-book-launches/

Additional Recommended Resources:

Join the *Write Your Story* Facebook group: https://www.facebook.com/groups/writeyourstorygroup/

HopeWriters Podcast: http://hopewriters.com/podcast/

National Novel Writing Month: https://nanowrimo.org/

Betsy Herman's blog: www.lovethatbetsy.com

Note: Any weblinks mentioned are active at the time of publication.

Other books by Betsy Herman

When Infertility Books Are Not Enough: Embracing Hope During Infertility

Does your desire for motherhood seem impossible? Have your hopes led to disappointment? Are you facing delayed dreams? What do you do with an empty womb and a broken heart? You've dreamed of being a mother ever since you were a young girl, but these dreams remain just that. Maybe you face secondary infertility, and your child does not yet know the joy of growing up with siblings. Or, perhaps you would like to gain some insight about this struggle to conceive, to help someone that you care about.

This is one woman's story. She's happily married, childless, in her mid-30's, and struggling to become pregnant. What does God have to say to her? Are there others fighting the battle to conceive as well, and what are their outcomes? How can her belief that God is good survive a still-empty womb?

Here is Betsy's story of the emotional roller coaster called infertility. Despite her pain and disappointment, she began to realize that God is for her and not against her. Throughout her challenging personal journey, Betsy shares her steadfast understanding that God is good, regardless of the circumstances. If you need encouragement in your delayed dreams, then this book is for you. You are not alone!

Seasons: A Picture Book

Children and adults alike will enjoy experiencing the four seasons from a child's perspective. While traversing spring, summer, autumn, and winter, readers are reminded of God's unchanging goodness regardless of what each season brings. These timeless, classic illustrations and rhyming lyrics will delight readers of all ages as it teaches children about the four seasons.

Made in the USA
Las Vegas, NV
13 November 2022